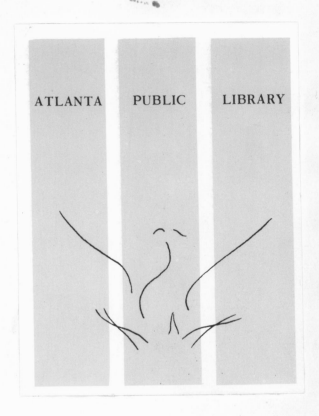

'TODAY WE WILL ONLY GOSSIP'

BEATRICE GLENAVY, 1905

'Today we will only Gossip'

by Beatrice Lady Glenavy

Constable London

First published in 1964
Second Impression 1964
by Constable and Company Ltd.
10-12 Orange Street, London WC 2
© Beatrice Glenavy 1964
Printed in Great Britain
by C. Tinling & Co. Ltd.
Liverpool, London and Prescot

B
Glenavy

For Patrick, Michael and Brigid

Contents

Contents

Illustrations

A*

Facing Page 129

John Hughes, from a water colour drawing by Walter Osborne
John Hughes in the Modelling Room, 1900

Facing Page 160

Mark Gertler, 1923
Samuel Beckett at his mother's knee
On the afternoon of the first day-light air-raid on London, July 17, 1917.

Facing Page 161

Katherine Mansfield, 9 Selwood Terrace, London, 1914
S. S. Koteliansky, James Stephens, Lady Ottoline Morrell, 10 Gower Street,
London, 1935

Facing Page 192

THE INTRUDER by Beatrice Glenavy, RHA, 1933
PRIMULA by Beatrice Glenavy, RHA, 1953

Facing Page 193

PAPER and THE DANCING MEN by Beatrice Glenavy, RHA, 1962

Acknowledgements

My grateful thanks are due to the late Mrs Cynthia Stephens for permission to use a poem, and a fragment of a poem, by James Stephens; also to Mr Thomas McGreevy for his beautiful little poem on page 152. Mrs Middleton Murry has been very kind in allowing me to use letters of John Middleton Murry. I want to thank the Estate of D. H. Lawrence, Laurence Pollinger Ltd. and William Heinemann Ltd., for permission to quote from the letters of D. H. Lawrence and Frieda Lawrence, and the Society of Authors, as the literary representative of the Estate of the late Katherine Mansfield, for permission to include her letters. Also Dilys Powell and Leonard Woolf for letting me use bits from their obituary notices about Kot. I remember with gratitude the late Susan Mitchell for her Arts Club ditty about me. There are others, whose names I do not know, who wrote ballads of 1916 such as, 'Kevin Barry' and 'de Valera had a cat' and Mr Harry Graham who wrote the lyric for the song about Augustus John on page 84.

I am also grateful to Miss Hilary Pyle and to Mr Terence de Vere White, Literary Editor of the *Irish Times*, for their very practical help. And to my son Michael Campbell and to Mr Bill Holden for their enduring encouragement. Finally I thank my friend Dr Monk Gibbon for all his valuable assistance and good advice.

I

Earliest recollections - Parents and forebears - Childhood at Carrickmines - We move to Foxrock - I show myself unregenerate

Except for some vague and fleeting impressions of people and places my first memory is of a newly built house standing in bare fields beside the Protestant church at Carrickmines. It was about the year 1888 and we had moved from the suburbs of Dublin where my elder sister Edna and my younger brother Philip and I were born. Carrickmines was then a wild and lonely place. The few large old houses were inhabited by people of the professional classes.

At first when we went there no one seemed anxious to know us because my father was 'in business'. I remember coming out of Sunday School hoping to make friends with the other children. A little girl said to me, 'We are not allowed to play with you because your father has a shop.' I was very impressed by this and felt it was rather distinguished for us to be set apart in this way.

We did not miss the company of other children for we had imaginary people whom we played with and we ourselves became imaginary people. My elder sister Edna did not take much part in our games. There was an attic at the top of the house in which there was a water cistern. She made this place her private domain and we were not allowed in. We did not know what she did there; she said she was composing music and inventing a new kind of musical instrument. The cistern used to make very queer gurgling noises which we supposed came from the new musical instrument.

We had a governess with the charming name of Lottie Miles who came daily by train to Carrickmines. She was young and rather nice-looking—she wore a man's high, hard collar and tie and always seemed to be suffering from a very bad cold in the head. She was very good to us and made the most wonderful rag dolls with painted faces and hands cut out of old white kid gloves.

13

One Christmas she gave us *The Adventures of Pinocchio*. This book, which years later became a children's classic, had just been translated from the original Italian and published in London. It was the first book that I remember and we all read and re-read it till we almost knew it off by heart.

On Sunday evenings my mother played hymns on the piano and we stood around her singing, 'Now the darkness gathers.' How sad and enjoyable it was! She taught us the names of the stars and the planets as we gathered at the nursery window on a clear frosty night. Their very names seemed full of the sense of space and eternity.

There were other nights when we sat huddled in the big bow-window of our nursery to watch a thunderstorm over the Three Rock Mountain. We waited for the flash and then counted the seconds till we heard the sound of thunder to find out how far away the storm was and whether it was coming nearer or going farther off. My father would say, 'A thunderstorm travels against the wind', and predict its behaviour; one almost felt he was in control of the elements.

Father had a great weather-sense and always seemed to know what the weather was going to do, whether the wind was going to change and where it was going to change to. Every spring a day came when he would say, 'Well, girls, if the wind blows tonight you'll have the cuckoos in the morning.' We found that this saying could be applied to other events besides the coming of the cuckoos. A night of storm was often the prelude to something lovely 'in the morning'.

My mother was the youngest of a family of seven; her taste in art and literature was of the period of the Pre-Raphaelite brother-hood. She had been a singer, but I hardly remember her voice for increasing deafness had put an end to her singing. What I do remember is her laughter; she had a gay, ringing laugh that made everybody else laugh too, even though they did not know what she was laughing at.

Mother's ancestors on both sides had been English, mostly Quakers, though she always spoke of herself as a 'Free-Thinker'. We all attended the Protestant church but she encouraged us to

14

question everything that we heard there. She used to quote Tennyson to us: 'There lives more faith in honest doubt, Believe me, than in half the creeds.' Mother's maiden name had been Theresa Moss and she was teaching music when my father first met her. She also had a talent for drawing. My sister Dorothy and I seemed to have inherited it; we were destined to go to the School of Art in Dublin as soon as we were old enough. My mother and her sister Annie had been there as young girls.

Annie had married a distinguished Scotsman, Dr Ramsay Traquaire, a Fellow of the Royal Society and an expert on fossil fishes. For a short time he had held an appointment in the Dublin Museum, where Annie had made drawings of fossils for him. When they went to live in Edinburgh she became well known there for what was spoken of in our family as 'your Aunt Annie's Art Work'. As well as bringing up a family she had painted murals in the song-school of St. Mary's Cathedral, also in the Catholic Apostolic Church and other buildings. Her 'Art Work' included embroidery, enamels and some very beautiful illuminated books.

My mother's eldest brother, Edward, had a great talent with his pencil and paint-brush. He had been a doctor in the Navy and went to the Arctic with Captain Nares on H.M.S. *Alert* in 1875 —he wrote and illustrated a very large and elaborate book about it all, called *Shores of the Polar Sea*. It was considered very precious and indeed it was a most impressive production; we were allowed to look at it on Sunday evenings.

From my mother's account of her family we grew up to look on them with a reverence amounting to awe. They all seemed to have distinguished themselves in one way or another in spite of the fact that after my grandfather's death his young wife had been left with very little money to bring up and educate a large family. Her second son, William, while still a small boy had gone to work in the offices of a Lancashire cotton-mill 'with a tin trunk and half a crown in his pocket'; he finally became head of his firm and very rich. He bought Pre-Raphaelite pictures and had 'the finest collection of *cloisonné* enamel outside the British Museum'.

The youngest son, Richard, became Registrar of the newly formed Royal Dublin Society which had its headquarters in Leinster House,

Kildare Street. He was also the Public Analyst and had a laboratory in Leinster House where he did some very valuable work with radon, which is a form of radium emanation. I remember going with my cousins to see this marvel—a small point of light glowing in a dark room.

My father thought that everything that my mother said and did was right. He had worked in his father's waterproof business in Dublin since he was sixteen years old. His people originally came from Spain. They were silk merchants named Alvarez who had first settled in England, where they changed their name to Elvery as that was the way it was pronounced there. We were interested in our Spanish ancestry, but Father knew very little about it. In England his father had married a Miss Catherine Jane Fuller, a direct descendant of the Reverend Thomas Fuller, D.D., the eminent historian and divine, author of *Worthies of England* and other works, but I think he took very little interest in his distinguished ancestor, and I believe we never had a copy of any of his 'works' in the house.

My mother was reading *Robert Elsmere* when we moved into our new house in Carrickmines, which she duly called 'Elsmere'. It was a very ordinary two-storey house without much character; the most pleasant room was the nursery looking south towards the Three Rock Mountain, and there was a large window on the landing with a border of coloured glass. We children used to amuse ourselves looking through the different colours at the garden outside. How terribly sad it was if you looked through the blue—so cold, remote and lonely! The green glass was almost as bad, and the red was frightening, like Hell Fire. Through the yellow, even if it was a grey day, the garden was full of sunshine—eternal summer. We jostled and pushed each other on the low window-seat, all trying to peep through the tiny bits of yellow glass.

The country round Carrickmines was beautiful. We knew every field and lane and hill in it; the best ponds for leeches, water-beetles and newts; the best streams for minnows and sticklebacks. We knew the best places for primroses, blackberries and mushrooms. We made dolls' knives, putting pins on the railway line near Carrickmines Station and lying in the long grass beside the track while the train roared over them. We held 'Pagan Rites' at the cromlech in the Druids' Glen, and when we found a dead bird we burnt it as a sacrifice on the Druids' Altar, while we danced round it, singing loudly.

Sometimes the nursemaid came with us with the baby, Ronald, in the perambulator. We were glad of her company when we went by a lane where there were encampments of tinkers, whom we were afraid of, or when there was a danger of encountering a terrifying man whom we called 'Shaky Head', whose head and whole body never stopped twisting and contorting as he walked. To see him in the distance was enough to start us running wildly for home.

The nursemaid's favourite walk was to Carrickmines Railway Station where she was having a flirtation with the porter. One day while we were there I altered the signals for the trains, which were worked by large levers on the platform. When the porter heard the clatter of the signal falling down he rushed at me and flung me into a sort of dungeon under a big water-tank, a place where all the paraffin lamps were kept. It had no windows and was pitch dark. I was terrified. I kept on screaming till he let me out.

One day my brother Philip and I saw a carriage of an unusual design moving towards us, *without* a horse! It was incredible; we stood fixed to the spot, stiff with astonishment. It passed us and roared away in the distance, and we ran madly home to tell everyone. They wouldn't believe us.

We had our own fields about the house at Carrickmines where my father kept some sheep and a couple of cows, and we also had fowls and turkeys. I had a white turkey for whom I built a house with stones and cement, with planks and sods for a roof. This house had a hall and one room where I put hay for a nest. The turkey laid eggs and hatched them out in her sitting-room, and I made a garden for her round her house. There was a large water-tank in the back yard with a wooden lid on which we played 'ship', and the wooden lid made a hollow sound when we walked on it, which we imagined was like walking on the deck of a ship. There was a hayloft, too, where we played smugglers in hiding.

17

I was normally the inventor of our games while the younger children sat round saying, 'Think of something.' One day I made a disastrous decision: that we should have a death among our dolls. We settled on Punch, one of Miss Miles's finest achievements. We put him in a cardboard box and carried it in a large black 'driving cloak' of my grandmother's to the end of the garden, chanting a funeral march. It was so painful that we were quickly reduced to a state of despair. We heaped the grave with flowers and returned to the house, where Dorothy wept so bitterly and we were all so miserable that I slipped away and ran back to the grave, unearthed Punch and returned with him, saying I had heard him calling me, he was not dead, he was only pretending and it was all a joke. I realized that death was too terrifying a mystery to introduce into our games.

Birth was also a great mystery. When the lambing season started we were astonished to see the birth of a lamb. My mother's maternity nurse had told us in answer to our inquiries that the Doctor brought the babies in his little black bag, so we naturally thought the same process applied to the arrival of lambs.

My father loved his garden and his game of golf. His life was devoted to the upkeep, the well-being and happiness of his family. If anyone spoke of the problem of wars, of international disturbances, or just domestic disagreements and difficulties, my father would say, 'In my humble opinion it all comes from the stomach.' Father played the cello—he had been a pupil of Herr Elsner, a German who had settled in Ireland and whose family did much in later years for music in his adopted land.

We had a lodger and family friend, Frank Browning, whom we children called 'Brown', and he played the violin. He and my mother and father used to play trios at night in a room under our nursery, and I remember nights of storm with the gales sweeping over the Dublin mountains when the sound of the wind seemed to be part of the music, wild and sad and rather frightening. It was good to feel that we were safely in bed with the nursery night-light burning in the basin on the wash-stand. On other nights 'Brown' used to practise the solo parts of violin concertos in his bedroom. We got to know the works of Beethoven, Mendelssohn and Max Bruch long before we knew who composed them.

My mother read a lot of poetry and must have passed it on to us. My mind was filled with Lancelot and King Arthur and *Sonnets from the Portuguese*—I became very romantic. I remember my first experience of thinking that I was in love. It was in a field at Carrickmines at a Sunday School Sports and I was about twelve years old. We had run races, our Sunday School prizes had been distributed, and before tea we stood round and sang a hymn— 'Safe in the arms of Jesus.' I shared a hymn-book with a very good-looking boy named Cecil Jones. The sun was shining, the summer's day was all around us, and looking at Cecil's hand beside mine holding the hymn-book I felt an ecstasy of happiness I have never forgotten.

I suppose all children are interested in remarks about their personal appearance made by their elders. I wonder, do they all carry these remarks about with them engraved on their hearts for the rest of their lives as I did? I remember my grandmother brushing my hair. I was sitting before a mirror and she looked at the reflection of my pale, freckled face in the glass and said, 'Ah, my dear child, your hair is your only beauty.' I found this thought very depressing. Another time our nursemaid said to me, 'Your eyes are like two little holes burned in a blanket.' I brooded over this and was sad, but consoled myself by thinking I still had my hair.

We moved to Foxrock, about a mile nearer Dublin, in 1896. My sister Marjorie and my brother Malcolm were born there. We were now quite a large family, seven children and 'Brown'. In the back garden at Foxrock 'Brown' built himself a workshop where he did carpentry and made things out of metal. He even made a machine which sent long electric flashes darting from one point to another. I and my brothers and sisters used to stand on glass jam-jars and hold on to something. When 'Brown' switched on his machine we became so full of electricity that our hair stood on end.

'Brown' was a great education to us. He took us to concerts and operas and gave me violin lessons. Sometimes we used to pester him, peeping through the window of his workshop asking, 'What are you making now?' He would reply, 'A caution for rattlesnakes and a crutch for lame ducks.' Though we enjoyed the operas and concerts, we seldom went to any lighter form of entertainment, so we were very excited when a neighbour at Foxrock suggested taking us with her own children to a pantomime. When my grandmother heard of it she was horrified and my mother refused the invitation on our behalf. She said, 'Your grandmother is so good to you. She makes all your flannel underclothes. You should do as she wishes.' How gladly would we have dispensed with the flannel underclothes!

We had a family of cousins who lived on the sea-front at Greystones in County Wicklow, and during the summer holidays I used to stay with them. It was delightful to be near the sea: there was bathing on the South Strand; there were boats in the harbour; we went spinning for mackerel or exploring the pools in the rocks in front of the house at low tide. Then there was the Cherry Orchard at Delgany with tea in a garden under the cherry trees on old wooden tables full of earwigs.

The highlights of my visits were the evenings when Mr Pepper's White Coons gave concerts on the front: they had a very small piano on a platform with an awning hung with Chinese lanterns. Mrs Pepper in a little straw boater and a shirt-waister with leg-of-mutton sleeves sang, 'De same old moon am shinin'.' She was the essence of beauty and elegance. My eldest cousin Claude stood beside her, also wearing a boater, and turned over her music. It was whispered among us that Claude was in love with Mrs. Pepper. Anyway, the moon really was shining and I sat with my cousin Arnold holding my hand, feeling that life had no more to offer.

One summer I came all ready for the usual round of happiness. My girl cousins met me at the station and told me all was changed. The Children's Special Service Mission had arrived. Three young men were looking after the boys and three young women had taken charge of the girls. I felt that what was happening was of great importance to my cousins.

We sang hymns and prayed on the beach. It was rather fun marching together singing Salvation Army hymns, but we spent so much time at Bible readings and prayer meetings that I began to long for the old unregenerate days. However, my girl cousins seemed infatuated by the principal Bible Lady. I can see her now in her plain black dress with tight sleeves, her full bosom in one solid curve from her neck to her waist, her little white collar and cuffs, her hair smooth and done in a bun at the back of her head, her face comely and full of religious peace and certainty.

We no longer went to hear the White Coons, but at least we still had the wonder of the sea. At the end of the Mission there was to be a farewell meeting in the schoolhouse. We went there in the late evening, the escalonia hedges heavy with perfume. The schoolhouse was dimly lit with one oil-lamp. Our Bible Lady spoke for a while; we prayed and sang a hymn. Then she asked us to kneel down and close our eyes; it was growing dark outside. I was beside one of the little latticed windows, and could hear the swallows screaming as they whirled round in their wild flight before settling down for the night. I could also hear the happy, jangling, raucous music from the merry-go-rounds, swings and side-shows at the harbour. Life outside the schoolhouse seemed entrancing.

The Bible Lady began telling us in a quiet voice that 'the Lord Jesus Christ was outside the door'. In a moment He would enter; we were to keep our eyes closed. He would walk up the centre of the room between the wooden benches and desks. Every girl who was ready to give herself to Him was to hold up her hand. There was silence for a moment. Then the Bible Lady began her running commentary. 'He is at the door. He is coming in.' No one moved. A couple of girls began to sob. The voice went on: 'He wants you to hold up your hand.' I could hear the rustle of the girls moving their hands up. 'He is looking at you. He is coming nearer.' The tension seemed unbearable. I felt that I was quite incapable of holding up my hand. Then it was all over. Another prayer and hymn and we quietly filed out into the night.

I was thirteen years of age. I think that my feelings were those of indignation at the unwarranted intrusion into my private life. I walked between my cousins in silence, then suddenly I felt they had slipped away. The Bible Lady had taken their place and she was talking softly and urgently. 'Why do you refuse Him? Why are you so cold and hard?' I could not speak. For one moment I

21

thought of striking her. She handed me a card and asked me to write to her if I change my mind and then she was gone. My cousins closed in again beside me. After that holiday I left Greystones feeling rather in disgrace because of my refusal to be saved.

There was a bush of verbena near the hall-door of my cousins' house in Greystones; we loved to pick a leaf when passing, crush it in our fingers and breathe its lovely fragrance. In the bathroom of that house there was always a cake of carbolic soap for the children to wash with. To this day the perfume of verbena or the smell of carbolic soap bring back vividly those summer days, the sea and the happy carefree holiday existence.

2

I go to the School of Art and widen my horizons - The
upbringing of a family 'in business' - At Miss Elsner's
academy - 'Hops' and horse-drawn cabs - George Moore
writes a story and I am flattered - John Hughes shocks the
Board of Education - Intellectual ferment in a provincial
capital - I converse with Mr Chesterton - Sarah Allgood unveils
a statue - Train journeys with Mr J. B. Yeats père -
Four ingénues in Paris - I find a beau and uncover a secret -
Nocturne in a sculptor's studio

It was a few years after I started to attend the Dublin Metropolitan School of Art that the South African War broke out. How thrilling it was to have a war! How interesting the newspapers were with names like Mafeking, Spion Kop, Botha, Kruger, de Wet! Buttons were sold in the shops bearing portraits of the British Generals, and we wore them on the lapels of our coats.

When I first went to the Art School I was put in the antique room 'to shade from the cast'. This was an awful process done with chalk and a chamois-leather stump and breadcrumbs. I took a long time to get an even shadow, pricking out the black spots and adding more black spots till my drawing gave a very realistic representation of a plaster cast. I worked hard but began to have doubts as to whether I was learning anything.

One day another girl took me to the modelling-room. I had never seen modelling-clay; it was a revelation. I took a piece and modelled a baby's head. My sister Marjorie was an infant at the time and I did it from my memory of her. John Hughes, who taught modelling, saw this effort and suggested that I should join his class, which I did and quickly became a star turn. John Hughes was a most amusing and inspiring teacher. He looked more like a Frenchman or an Italian than an Irishman; perhaps that was due to his great love of those countries. He talked to us about everything, and his lively mind was a great pleasure to his students.

In the painting class at the other end of the School William Orpen, who was then eighteen years of age, was the star. I was five years his junior. He had been there some years and was just leaving to go to the Slade School in London.

As I began to meet new people I was fascinated to find that they often held very different views on religion and politics from those of my own family. My father was shocked when I told him there were people in the School of Art who were actually 'pro-Boer'. He found it difficult to conceive of anyone being 'anti-British'. He was most distressed when I said I had met people who thought Ireland should have Home Rule. It was as if I was getting into bad company.

When I was sixteen I got a three-week scholarship to the South Kensington School of Art. Before I went, my father said he wanted to warn me about some dangers I might encounter. I was embarrassed, as I thought he was going to talk about men. But he only wanted to tell me about a cousin of ours who had gone to England and become a Roman Catholic, and, later, a nun. I think both my parents were very innocent. Perhaps we were all innocent in those days.

When the time came for Dorothy to start her career as an artist she decided to go to the Royal Hibernian Academy's School in Abbey Street where there was a very good teacher of painting, Walter Osborne, who could not believe when he saw her first efforts that she had never painted from life before. John Hughes used to speak of having 'the clever Miss Elvery' in his class; but Walter Osborne would say that he had 'the cleverer Miss Elvery' in his. At that time Edna, who was a pupil of Michele Esposito in the Royal Academy of Music, had also been designated a 'clever Miss Elvery'; and as Marjorie grew up, she too showed musical talent.

My father was finding it rather difficult to afford to start Philip and Ronald in professional careers as well as sending Malcolm to a good public school. Because of the still-prevailing social attitude towards people 'in business' my mother was determined that her sons should not go into my father's shop. We older girls had managed to carry on our education by winning scholarships and prizes but Marjorie never seemed to have the opportunity of getting in touch with such things. She had many other talents besides music—she had written some deeply tragic and desolate poems by the age of nine and had played hockey for Ireland by the age of seventeen.

I was at the School of Art five days a week. On Saturday mornings I went to a private school at the end of our road run by Herr Elsner's daughter Ida for languages and piano lessons. I was no linguist, but I worked hard at the piano. There was certainly nothing dull or ordinary about Ida Elsner's method of teaching. During my piano lessons she used to do the house-work, leaving the door open so that she could hear if I struck a wrong note. She would yell down from an upstairs room, 'B flat!', or whatever it should have been, to correct me. One day when Ida was out, a sister of Mrs Elsner's who was also a teacher of music took my lesson. I went through my scales and exercises and then my Grieg pieces. She sat in absolute silence. When I had finished she said, 'Ach, Ida will make somethink out of you.' I was overwhelmed by the prospect of becoming a pianist as well as a sculptor.

In spite of the storms and stresses of growing up, our life at our home in Foxrock was a happy one. After supper on Sunday evenings we sat round the table and sang part-songs. My father had a fine bass voice but, for some strange reason, when he sang his eyes poured with tears. We always found this very amusing. My mother had become stone deaf, but she had finally accepted her deafness and sat smiling and knitting, glad to see us all enjoying ourselves. We had all learnt to speak to her on our fingers and, like Beethoven, she always kept a notebook near her for people to write in.

When my brother Philip started his medical course in the Royal College of Surgeons we had many young visitors from the Medical School. We went to dances in Dublin. This meant a long, slow, cold drive from Foxrock in a horse-drawn cab, the inside of which smelt as if the horse had been stabled in it. The dances we went to were usually subscription 'hops' in the Old Aberdeen Hall of the Gresham Hotel.

25

We were fortunate in having some very good dancing partners among our medical student friends, and we kept very much in our own party at our own table. To stand up and be taken into the arms of a young man and become one Perfect Being, gliding away down the long dance floor to the solemn, almost religious, strains of the Choristers' Waltz—to be guided, reversed, halted and swept on again, without speaking, was a rapture; an ecstasy very hard to describe. It was like the beauty of hearing Mrs Pepper singing 'De same ole moon am shinin' '—only more so.

I do not remember that we drank anything but tea or coffee, perhaps lemonade or some sort of wine-cup, nor do I remember our young men drinking. We heard of them going on 'binges', but this was not while they were with us. Dancing in those days was not solely romantic and spiritual. There were grand romps in the Lancers, when two couples would form a circle and the men would keep their feet on the ground going madly round and round, while the girls' feet and their long skirts flew out and swept round in the air. The nights usually ended up with 'D'ye ken John Peel' and a wild gallop up and down the ballroom. Then there was the long drive home in the horse-drawn cab. My father always sat up till we had arrived back; he could never sleep till all his children were safely in bed. This rather detracted from the pleasure of our evening, but we could not persuade him to do otherwise.

About this time George Moore, who was living in Ely Place, published his book of short stories with an Irish setting. It was called *The Untilled Field*. It had been written, Moore said, in order 'that Ireland's future writers should have models'. It was to be his service to the great cause that Douglas Hyde and Yeats and Lady Gregory and so many others had at heart. In his preface to a later edition Moore says, 'As fast as these stories were written they were translated into Irish and published in a very pretty book of which nobody took any notice, and that the Gaelic League could not be persuaded to put in its window.'

In the original edition of *The Untilled Field* are two stories about a sculptor and his model, 'In the Clay' and 'The Way Back', afterwards amalgamated into a single tale called 'Fugitives'. The sculptor in these stories is a good portrait of Hughes. In 'Fugitives' an Irish priest commissions a statue of the Virgin. The sculptor has great difficulty in finding a model. When Moore's story appeared the gossips of Dublin went so far as to suggest that the model in the story was drawn from me. I was flattered and pleased, although the actual plot of the story has nothing to do with me.

Since those far-off days modelling in clay has gone out of fashion; to a student of today Hughes's teaching, in which we had to keep in close touch with the model and avoid all distortion, would seem absurd. Hughes impressed on us the fact that modelling was drawing, drawing all the time. Each slight move of the turntable on which the model was posing must correspond with a turn of the clay model that we were working on. Nor was it only the straight view which must be considered; we must look at the sections, the model seen from above and below. We must also *love* the thing we were working at, the articulation of the elbow or the knee. He would make us examine the model close up, to see how wonderfully and beautifully he or she was made.

We had a young male model, an Italian born in Dublin. Instead of retiring into the models' cubby-hole in the corner of the room during the rests, Hughes encouraged him to associate freely with the students; he didn't really need any encouragement. Hughes said we must watch the human figure in movement; watch it all the time, not only while the model was posing. So during the rests we all sat on the hot pipes together. When the Inspector of the Board of Education came round, this behaviour led to some shocked comments. Hughes received an official instruction saying that the nude models were not to associate with the young lady students. Hughes was very angry and replied that he considered it part of the young ladies' artistic education to become familiar with the naked human form. The Board of Education decided to leave us alone.

In those days Dublin was a city full of intellectual and artistic activity. Yeats and Lady Gregory were creating a national theatre. I remember seeing one of the first performances of *Cathleen ni Houlihan* in St Teresa's Hall. Maud Gonne was Cathleen. She looked like a very elderly goddess and came through the door of the cottage bent nearly double, the stage being so small and the door of the set so low. Her great height made the other actors

27

look like pigmies. This was before the generous Miss Horniman presented them with the premises later to become famous as the Abbey Theatre.

Playwrights sprang into being overnight. George Russell ('AE'), painter and economist, and Sir Horace Plunkett were spreading the gospel of co-operative farming which because of Russell's special interest in the Creameries was to make Ireland a land flowing with 'cream and honey'. Michele Esposito, pianist, composer and conductor, had his Dublin Orchestral Society, and the Feis Ceoil was beginning to discover young singers and musicians of the calibre of John McCormack. Everyone seemed to be doing something for Ireland, and without shedding a drop of their own or anyone else's blood.

Hugh Lane had his dream of building a gallery to span the Liffey and house the wonderful collection of pictures he was buying to present to his native land. George Moore was living in Ely Place and writing *Hail and Farewell*. The United Arts Club had an odd and amusing collection of talented members including Percy French, composing and singing his delightful songs.

Sarah Purser was starting a Co-operative Stained Glass Studio, to try to keep in Ireland part of the huge sum of money which went every year to Germany for church windows. As a young woman she had worked in Julien's *atelier* in Paris about the year 1880; she is mentioned in the Journal of Marie Bashkirtseff, was a friend of Berthe Morisot and Louise Breslau, and worked in Ireland as a portrait painter for many years, becoming very well known and much sought after. She had a fine old Georgian house in Dublin, with two large drawing-rooms where she entertained her friends to tea once a month on her 'At Home' Day.

Sarah Purser was disappointed if there were fewer than fifty people at these gatherings, and used to boast of how many sandwiches she could make out of a few herrings to put before her visitors. She had the reputation of being very rich and very mean, and carefully fostered this idea of her meanness, speaking of her family as the 'pinching parsimonious Pursers'. I only remember her generosity. It was she who first introduced me to the world of art and drama in Dublin while I was still very young.

Sarah Purser's 'At Home' Day was the only remaining salon in the city which retained the tradition of a society rapidly passing away—an Anglo-Irish salon with an international atmosphere. Her witty and caustic tongue was as sharp and pointed as Swift's; indeed, she was in the tradition of Swift, and could not tolerate humbug or bear patiently with platitudes. Her sense of justice and her courage prompted her in her young days to advance Irish art, industry and music; anything that would promote the idea of beauty in her native land. She was a Nationalist when most of her friends were Unionists. She was a firm Parnellite and did not care whom she offended in defence of the Leader.

My job on Sarah Purser's 'At Home' Days was to hand tea and cake to the visitors and to talk to the old ladies seated round the outskirts of the storm of conversation, which was usually conducted standing up by the younger people in the centre of the floor. On one of her Days she had both Bernard Shaw and G. K. Chesterton. As a great treat I was introduced to Chesterton. We both seemed to be at a loss for something to say, so I plunged into telling him how much I and my sisters had enjoyed *The Man who was Thursday*, and how, while we were reading it, my father had bought a new kind of sofa called a 'Chesterfield', and we decided, in honour of him, to call it a 'Chesterton' instead. He was laughing in a high squeaky way when Miss Purser came and took him away.

Chesterton and Shaw were in Dublin for a debate at the Abbey Theatre. I remember going to it and hearing Shaw talking at length, a tall Paganini-like figure on the bare stage. Seated round a table were Chesterton and several other people. Shaw was talking about bread, how it should be as much public property as the streets one walked in. A man in the pit got up and asked why Mr Shaw didn't speak of something that really mattered, like the seven hundred years of English oppression of the Irish people. Shaw paused for a second, then arms folded, stepped forward to the edge of the stage; a long arm shot out, one finger extended admonishingly. He said, 'Mark my words, *God is not mocked*. As surely as the ichthyosaurus disappeared from the face of the earth, so will man cease to exist if he is unable or unwilling to adapt himself to his surroundings.'

We were left to infer that people who talked endlessly about past oppression served no useful purpose in a changing world.

There was something almost like magic in the creation by Yeats and Lady Gregory of the original Abbey Theatre Company. Such a remarkable lot of talented people all together, at the same time, in the same place. How proud Yeats was of his leading lady, Sara Allgood, and how gracious and charming she was at Miss Purser's tea parties. Yeats said, 'She acts as well off the stage as on the stage.'

Oliver Sheppard, the sculptor, modelled a large imaginary heroic bust of James Clarence Mangan, which was put up in St Stephen's Green. A small group of interested onlookers were at the unveiling, which was done by Sara Allgood who, after a short ceremony, stood up on a seat and spoke Mangan's poem about himself:

> Roll forth, my soul, like the rushing river,
> That sweeps along to the mighty sea;
> God will inspire me while I deliver
> My soul of thee.

It might have been embarrassing—a young woman standing up on a seat in a public park speaking poetry—but she did it perfectly (the poem is fourteen verses long). People walking through the Green, children chasing each other, all stood to listen. She held us spellbound, while her lovely contralto speaking voice rolled forth with the story of the poet's tragic life, his loneliness, darkness, suffering and despair. As she finished the last lines—

> He, too, had tears for all souls in trouble,
> Here and in Hell

—it was almost a shock to find oneself among the flower-beds and the duck-ponds of St Stephen's Green.

In the years while I was going to the School of Art the Yeats family lived a few stations nearer Dublin than we did. Sometimes on his way to his studio the elder J. B. Yeats would get into my compartment in the train; I was usually reading something to educate myself! He would take my book and give a lecture on it to the railway carriage full of schoolchildren, much to their amusement and delight. Some years later when the two Miss Yeats, Lolly and Lilly, were running the Cuala Press they brought out a set of 'Broadsides' with black-and-white drawings by Jack Yeats, illustrations to ballads and poems, which were hand-coloured. These 'Broadsides' came out once a month for seven years and contained some of the best things that Jack Yeats ever did. I find his later paintings more like the work of a magician than a painter. I feel I have to fight against their power to cast a spell.

John Hughes had a studio in Lennox Street where he worked as a sculptor when he was not teaching at the School of Art. In 1903 he was given a commission, which was financed by public subscription, for a large monument to Queen Victoria to stand in Dublin. He gave up teaching and went to live in Paris as that city afforded greater facilities for carrying out such a big task; it was also the city where he had always longed to be. The modelling-room was a dull place without him, and his talk, which ranged over every subject with a sort of humorous wisdom.

During a summer holiday after John Hughes had gone Dorothy and I decided, with the help of one of my scholarships, to go to Paris for a few weeks. Two of our fellow art students were coming too—Cissie, who was the only girl in a large family named Beckett (one of her brothers became the father of Sam Beckett, the author of *Waiting for Godot*), and Stella, who was a sister of a brilliant medical student friend, Bethel Solomons, who later became the distinguished gynaecologist.

We went to Paris and stayed at a rather grim hotel in the Boulevard Montparnasse. We used to eat at a little café across the road. There we noticed a beautiful girl who was obviously English. The woman who owned the café told us that this girl was a Miss Kathleen Bruce, an art student.

One day a young man in the uniform of an English naval officer was with her. This young man was Scott of the Antarctic, who had just been promoted to the rank of Captain in the Royal Navy. He had already been on a National Antarctic Expedition to the South Pole on the *Discovery*. We were very interested in these two young people, they were so good-looking and so obviously in love. They were married a couple of years later, and in 1909 he organized the Antarctic Expedition which was to end in tragedy for all of them.

While we were in Paris we spent the mornings drawing from life in Colorossie's and in the afternoons wandered about sight-seeing, finding Paris very hot and exhausting. Before Dorothy and I and the other girls went on this continental trip we imagined that all Frenchwomen were beautiful and had lovely clothes; we were disappointed to find that they seemed to be small and sallow and plainly dressed. Perhaps the Boulevard Montparnasse was not quite the right quarter for what we were looking for.

One night we went to *Tristan* at the Opera House. We had a tiny box under the roof, from which we had a glimpse of the stage miles below. During the interval we went down and walked with the crowds in the large lovely foyer. Suddenly I saw a tall, fair-haired girl in a white dress coming towards us. I was immediately struck by her appearance, and was just going to exclaim to the others when I saw she was walking beside Dorothy, Stella and Cissie. There was a large mirror in front of us and it was myself I had seen. We all looked remarkable, for that matter : Stella was tall and dark and very good-looking; Dorothy was pretty and very fair with a long plait of yellow hair hanging down her back; Cissie's appearance was more maternal—in fact, she was once alluded to as our mother by the woman who owned our café, which was distressing for her as she was very little older than the rest of us.

Sarah Purser had a nephew about whom I had felt romantic. He was interested in music and books and pictures, and had gone to study at the Sorbonne. We had been writing letters about art and music to each other for some time and he had asked me to call on him when I came to Paris. We were to go out to lunch somewhere. Of course, I arrived too early. I am always too early for everything. I climbed up miles of stone stairs in some big building for students, only to find that he was in his dressing-gown and just about to shave. I said I did not mind waiting. He retired into his bedroom and I sat and looked around. I noticed with what perfect taste everything in his room was arranged, even to a pair of pale chamois-leather gloves near some mauve tulips. There was a writing-table covered neatly with papers—he hoped to become a writer—

32

Mr and Mrs William Elvery,
the author's parents, 1888

A group taken at an
Exhibition of the work of
Young Irish Artists,
Dublin, 1903:

back row
The Count Markiewicz;

second row
Cissie Beckett,
Dorothy Elvery,
Frieda Perrott;

third row
Lilly Williams,
Beatrice Elvery;

fourth row
Estella Solomons

W. B. Yeats with Sara Allgood, 1911

W. B. Yeats with Mrs George Russell at St Columba
College, Rathfarnham, Co. Dublin, about 1911

Captain Foster and Tom Casement in the
store of the Coast Life Saving Service in
Fleet Street, Dublin, 1923

and over it there was a dark patch on the faded wall, which looked as if a picture had lately been removed. When my escort came out of his room, all ready for lunch, I asked him, 'Where is the photograph which was hanging on that spot?' He looked very surprised, but pulled out a drawer and handed me a picture, with an affectionate inscription, of a very pretty girl with a guitar. He said, 'How did you know?' I said that in such a perfect room the mark on the wall was only too obvious. At that he laughed and I asked him why he had removed it. He did not seem to have any reason except that it might be more pleasant for us to meet if it was not there, and said the incident would almost make a short story. We pondered how the story should end. I suggested that the girl should pull out the drawer softly, find the photograph, carefully hang it up in its place, and then slip quietly away.

I went to Chartres with my young man from the Sorbonne. I suppose I was very impressed by the glass and the sculpture, but my chief memory is of having lunch in a restaurant where the waiter looked from one of us to the other and then addressed me as 'Madame'. I remember feeling very important and secure; a sort of married feeling. In the train on our way back to Paris I felt even more married when my companion fell asleep. There was a good-looking young Frenchman at the other end of the railway carriage; he looked at the sleeping figure and then at me, raised his eyebrows and shook his head sadly. I turned away and looked steadily out of the window.

One evening I had been to see John Hughes at his flat, where he lived with his sister and his dog Ned. He walked back with me to my hotel. On the way we went into his studio where he was working on one of the great clay models of the allegorical groups for the Queen Victoria monument. It was dark; it was late. He lit a candle and we examined the figures by the dim light. He put fresh damp cloths on his models. The bit of candle was very small, and as we sat and talked for a few minutes it flared up and went out. We both remained absolutely still, in silence. The dog was asleep on the floor and snoring gently. There was a faint sound of water dripping from a tap in the far corner of the studio. As my eyes got used to the darkness, the skylight window seemed to get

B

brighter and a few stars appeared. After what seemed quite a long time, during which neither of us had moved or spoken a word, Hughes got up and went to the door and opened it. The light from the boulevard streamed in. The dog got up and stretched himself and we went out.

Years later, after the war, when I went to Paris and met Hughes again and we walked and talked in the Luxembourg Gardens, I asked him if he remembered the night the candle went out. He said he did, paused for a minute, and then, with a quizzical look on his face, added, 'If you had laid a finger on me that night, my dog Ned would have flown at your throat and torn you limb from limb.' At that we both had to laugh; Hughes was a lovely person to laugh with and the relationship between him and myself was one of warm sympathetic friendship. It was also on my side one of complete devotion to a beloved master.

Hughes is forgotten today. Some years after Ireland achieved independence his monument to Queen Victoria was taken down, and the figures and stonework were stored in an old disused building which had once been a military hospital.

I made a feeble effort to get the two groups and the figure of Victory used separately, for they had no political significance apart from the statue of Victoria and could not have given offence to anyone. They would have looked splendid under the trees in the People's Gardens, but no one was interested in this idea. The monument was a fine piece of decoration; rich and strong in modelling, ornate and rather elaborate in design. It deserved a better fate.

3

I sit for Orpen - Character and comrades of a painter - Sarah
Purser builds me a shack - I try my hand at many arts - Stained
glass at ninepence the hour - A poet is rebuked and a
novelist vanquished - I draw a dead patriot

Orpen and I hardly spoke to each other while he was still a student
at the Art School. Each was interested in the other but we
were too shy to get better acquainted. Several of the girls I knew
were in love with him, and I found this rather amusing until I too
succumbed to the boyish charm and the great talent.

He once threw a bit of modelling-clay at me. It stuck in my hair
and I was thrilled at this special mark of attention. After he went
to London we used to hear of his successes and of how he was
establishing himself as a painter, and later we learnt of his marriage to Grace Knewstub, whose sister had married William Rothen-
stein.

It was some time after Orpen's marriage that he began to teach
at the Dublin School of Art. He was living in London but he came
over for a fortnight twice a term, for he was sentimental about
Ireland and devoted to his parents who were still in Stillorgan
where he was born. During these visits we began to get to know
each other better, and one day he asked me to sit for him. He had
a room in the School which he used as a studio.

Augustus John had just painted his 'Smiling Woman', and when
Orpen came to Dublin on this occasion he said, 'Everyone in London
is painting "Smiling Women".' So, with my hair hanging down my
back, his hat on my head, with feathers, scarves and bangles, he
produced two more smiling women. The first, to which he gave the
not wholly appropriate title of 'The Colleen', was sold at once and
he did a second one the next time he came. He worked very fast,
completely concentrated on his work and oblivious of his surroundings.

I loved these sittings and the lunches in Jammet's which followed them. This famous Dublin restaurant was at that time in its original site in St Andrew's Street. Orpen's visits to Dublin became festivals for his friends, as he was very generous and spent money lavishly. There were fantastic picnics in the Dublin mountains, lunches and dinners in Jammet's, bathing parties at Howth and on Portmarnock beach, and drives all over the country in Gogarty's big butter-coloured Rolls-Royce, one of the first cars of its kind to appear in Ireland.

Oliver Gogarty was one of Orpen's boon companions. Gogarty was a wit, scholar, raconteur, surgeon; a creator of limericks and of exquisite verse. His brilliant talk flew from one subject to another, from one unique epigram to some cuttingly witty comment and back to poetry and more poetry. It was difficult to keep up with him! Those times boasted other wits and writers of extraordinarily clever and sometimes very indelicate verse—Dublin was rich in table-talk of a very high and rare order.

Because of Orpen's early start at the Art School he had never had much general education. He was not interested in literature, music or ideas, but he had a great respect for the scholarship of his more erudite companions.

Another of Orpen's friends was William Sinclair, the man whom Cissie Beckett, Sam Beckett's aunt, had married. For some reason or other he was always known as 'the Boss'. It is hard to describe Cissie's husband except by saying he was a very 'colourful personality'. He had a certain amount of natural charm but he tried to invest himself with an outsize Walt Whitman-like quality. The result of this was more comic than impressive. He was a better person when he was just being himself.

In Orpen's book *Stories of Old Ireland and Myself* he writes of 'The Boss', saying, 'During the day he spent his time in Nassau Street dealing in antiques—and hating the job like poison. At heart "the Boss" or "the Beard" or "Sink" as we used to call him was an artist. He hated things so much that he hated people buying them, and he loved things so much that he hated to let them go—so as a dealer he was a failure. But as a friend he was a glorious success.'

Orpen was very humble about his talent, saying, 'I am not fit to

tie Augustus John's shoe-laces.' He never gave himself artistic airs
or dressed like an artist. In fact, he managed to look more like a
successful jockey than a painter. John Hughes said of him, 'He
has enough talent for six painters.' In London Orpen was beset by
people clamouring for their portraits to be painted. He was a hard
and conscientious worker and I think he turned to Ireland as a
respite from hard work.

As a teacher Orpen brought about a revolution in the life-class.
The students were allowed to talk and smoke. As it was almost
impossible to get a female model for the nude in Dublin he brought
girl models from London. Some of them added much to the social
life of the Bohemian element in the city.

For years Orpen and I kept up a correspondence. His letters as
well as mine were full of illustrations. He called me 'Bridgit' and
himself 'Digit' and had once signed a drawing: 'To Bridgit from the
lad who Digit.' Another time he signed a drawing: 'From the lad
who won't grow up.' I think he never wanted to grow up; his
letters were flowing over with high spirits, impish fun, jokes and
nonsense. When Orpen went to live in London he became a 'man of
the world', but behind it all was the little boy. I remember walking in Dublin with him; some ragged boys were kicking a ball
along the gutter and suddenly Orpen joined them and went wildly
kicking the ball down the middle of the street, with all the ragged
boys running and yelling round him.

Orpen always spoke of his mother with great affection, and I
felt there was a very deep relationship between them. He used to
say that the only real love was that between a parent and a child.
Old Mrs. Orpen was one of the most beautiful old ladies I ever saw,
she knew exactly what to do with ribbons and laces and little
side-curls, and Orpen's father was a handsome and distinguished-
looking old gentleman. Orpen painted a portrait group of them
sitting beside a little table; on the wall behind them is a round
mirror in which there is a reflection of the painter himself at
work.

Orpen's mother died during one of his visits to Dublin. After
her funeral he rang me up and we met. He said, 'Don't be sad
for me. All my life I have been haunted by the thought that some-

day she would have to die; the extraordinary thing is that now I feel a queer sense of relief.'

When I gave up going to the School of Art, Sarah Purser, who was always ready to help young artists, built a corrugated-iron studio in the yard of her Stained Glass Works. One day before I left the School, Orpen came into the modelling-room and said, 'Give up all this messing about with clay, get a canvas, come up to the life-class and I will make a painter out of you.' But I thought my fate was wrapped up in clay and I did not take advantage of his offer. I have often regretted this. I might have become a good painter and I might never have taken to making stained-glass windows, an activity which never gave me any pleasure.

In my tin studio I started to carry out some orders for busts. They were all well modelled but, I would say now, rather ordinary. So was a large relief of Mourning Victory which was to be erected in Clonmel Barracks Yard in memory of the officers and men of the Royal Irish Regiment who were killed in the South African War. Orpen's architect brother Richard designed the setting for this bronze relief.

During the 'Troubles', the Barracks at Clonmel were burnt down. I have no idea what became of my work. I grew to dislike busts because there never seems to be any place in an ordinary house to put them. Statuettes are just as bad, and I came to the conclusion that sculpture should either be huge and out in the open air against the sky or something small that you could hold in your hand like a Tanagra figure. I used to take little clay models to a place in a back-street in Dublin where a man made clay pipes. He put my models in his kiln with the pipes. My clay was not very suitable for firing and the models used often to 'fly'. Clay pipes were beginning to go out of fashion then because people were starting to smoke cigarettes, and so the clay-pipe maker closed down. I found that the expense of sending things to Paris or Belgium to be cast in bronze was so great that it was impossible to make a penny out of modelling.

I illustrated children's books; I made drawings for doctors of dissections and operations; I worked for silversmiths and drew archaeological finds for the museum. I also did some teaching, but the payment was very small. I cherished some faint hope of going to work in Paris. John Hughes had said, 'You must learn to cut stone.' He spoke of Rodin's studio and of the students he knew who were working there. My parents were horrified at the thought. Also, with such a large family, there was not much money to spare.

My father seemed to think that for a young girl 'going to Paris' was going to something worse than death. In every way he tried to dissuade me, saying, 'If you go to Paris, who will help your mother with the children?' and adding 'If you go to Paris it will break your grandmother's heart.' I think these arguments carried little weight with me. I had heard George Moore say something about women 'taking their art lightly as if across a fan', and John Hughes had said, 'Women can be great queens or great courtesans but they seldom become great creative artists.' I did not think I had much chance of becoming a great queen or a great courtesan and the possibility of becoming a creative artist of any importance seemed just as remote. I decided to stay at home.

Sarah Purser suggested that I should do stained glass. Orders were pouring in and she wanted workers. She had imported a stained glass artist from London and made him her manager. This manager also taught the craft of stained glass in the School of Art and I went back to the stained glass school to learn all about the fourteen processes. I became an employee at the Stained Glass Studio at a wage of ninepence an hour. I put away my clay and my modelling-stands and used my tin studio as a place for drawing cartoons for windows; all the other parts of window-making I did in the large Stained Glass Studio across the yard.

Sarah Purser had also got a skilled cutter and glazier from London, and there were several Irish boy apprentices and about four or five designers and painters. As we were being paid by the hour there was a lot of 'going slow' in the cutting and glazing part of the shop, where cricket and football were played with great gusto, whenever the manager was out, with a ball made of rolled-up newspapers. Quite a lot of time was also spent studying form in horse-racing. I worked so fast that Sarah Purser decided to pay me by the job. Otherwise I only got about a quarter of the pay of the other artists. If I was having a window cut I kept the cutter so hard at work that he would cry, 'You're turning this place into a blooming sweated industry.'

There was one amusing boy, Tommy Kinsella. He had come from a slum tenement and had sold newspapers in the street. He was very interested in the theatre and acting, and he and I became great friends. Sarah Purser found out about the 'going slow' and decided to give the staff a talking-to. The artists were not included in the meeting, so next morning I asked Tommy what had happened. He told me how Sarah Purser had arrived and called them into the office. They stood round her and she said (according to Tommy), 'If youse have tears to shed prepare to shed them now.' She then explained to them the principles of a co-operative workshop and gave them a good scolding on the iniquity of wasting time.

I did many windows during my years at the Stained Glass Studio. I think my best ones are a Good Samaritan in Carrickmines and a Crucifixion in a tiny church on Tory Island. They are rather like coloured illustrations to a child's book. I never got the right feeling for glass or the detached, austere quality necessary for ecclesiastical art.

I have always found it difficult to work in a dirty or untidy place. It was impossible to cope with the disorder of the large studio where we painted the glass, and the rest of the staff found my efforts to keep the place clean and tidy very amusing. A woman came in once a week to wash the floor, but except for the unpleasant smell left by this activity the place was much the same as before.

Our English manager, Mr Child, was not a very tidy man. One day when he was away in the country on business, I turned out, swept, tidied and dusted his office, sorting out the rubbish and burning it. No one took any notice of my efforts till an occasion when Sarah Purser was talking to some people about stained glass. Evie Hone had been working in the shop for some time, and they were all enthusiastic about her wonderful use of colour and the profound religious feeling expressed by her rather primitive kind of drawing. During the talk Sarah Purser suddenly turned to me and said, 'The best job of work you ever did (for a split-second I wondered which of my masterpieces she was going to mention) was on the day you cleaned out Mr Child's study.' The people she was talking to looked rather surprised and I had to laugh. I was glad that my great work had been approved of and noticed by her.

Sarah Purser and Lady Gregory were never on very friendly terms. One of the first windows I ever did was for the nuns at Gort where Lady Gregory lived, and I had been left to deal with the order myself. The nuns were charming. They showed me pictures of the subject and told me exactly how they wanted it done. It was to be a two-light window with the Blessed Margaret Mary on one side and Our Lord on the other.

I was working on the cartoon in my studio, when W. B. Yeats and Lady Gregory appeared. They looked at my drawing but said nothing. I began to explain that it was not quite the way I would like to have dealt with the subject but I had to do it the way the nuns wanted and showed them the pictures that the nuns had left with me. At that time W. B. Yeats was editing an occasional review called *Samhain*. The next edition of this magazine appeared with an article by Yeats saying that Miss Purser's Stained Glass Works was going the way of all artistic ventures in Ireland —it had started with the highest standards and ideals and was quickly descending to the lowest.

Yeats had mentioned my name and the cartoon that I was working on and Sarah read this and came flying to me in a terrible rage —what had I said to Yeats and Lady Gregory? I told her, and I heard afterwards that she demanded a denial of the statement in the article, an apology and, I think, the extermination of the entire review. She said, 'I don't interfere with your Abbey Theatre. Keep off my Stained Glass Works!'

George Moore was a constant visitor at Miss Purser's house. He also used to call at the Stained Glass Studio, whenever we had some finished window on view. He and Sarah used to have fierce verbal fencing matches of which I cannot remember a word except that she nearly always got the better of him. On one occasion he spoke of someone as 'that woman'. She corrected him, saying,

'That lady', at which he replied haughtily, 'All women are ladies to me.'

On another occasion in my tin studio at the Stained Glass Works, after some fierce exchanges had passed between Sarah and Moore, he started to walk away, looking rather beaten and pathetic with his little sloping shoulders and mincing steps. Sarah had turned to speak to me about something else when an idea occurred to her. She dashed to the door and called out to him, 'Now go round Dublin and repeat all my *bons mots* and pretend that they are your own.' His retreating figure paused; he looked angrily over his shoulder and continued on his way.

In May 1906, when I was still at the Stained Glass Works, Sarah came in one day and said I was going to a nursing-home where Michael Davitt the Irish patriot was lying dead. I was to make a drawing of him. I duly took my drawing-board, paper, pencil and rubber and went to the home. The Matron brought me into the room where he lay; she was evidently a great admirer of his. She told me how he had been sentenced to fifteen years' penal servitude for his activities in the Fenian movement in Ireland. As a young man he had lost an arm through a machinery accident in a cotton factory in Lancashire; and while he was in Portland Gaol he had been harnessed to a cart which carried stones. He was released from gaol seven years later. She then left me alone and closed the door after her.

The silence and stillness were almost paralysing. I felt I had to make a great effort to pull myself together and get to work. I drew for about an hour. The window was open. It was spring. A couple of times the curtain blew in gently. I started with fright; that anything should move seemed terrifying. My drawing was not much good, and when I had finished it the Matron returned and took it away. I think it was given to Michael Davitt's widow who was lying ill in the same nursing-home. I never heard anything more about it.

A few years earlier Orpen had painted a portrait of Davitt and during one of the sittings he had said to Orpen, 'You are young. Take my advice. Don't take any side. Just live and learn to try to understand the beauties of this wonderful world that God has been good enough to give us to live in. There is nothing that spoils its beauty more than party politics and intrigues or taking sides in any war against your fellow men. These things have ruined this beautiful world for me for years and years. Aye, take my advice. Live to love and never hurt a flea when he bites you. Remember it's his nature; he is only answering his call to live and love with as much right as you or I.'

4

Carrickmines Church furnishes me a suitor - A speedy
proposal and a long engagement - Two sisters find solace in
song - Dusk in York Minster - Sarah Purser tracks down a
collateral - Sam Beckett poses for a painting - Sister Dorothy
is married - I decide to go to London - George Moore is
pilloried and I am praised - Goings-on at the Slade - Professor
Tonks speaks of me - I bandy quotations with George
Moore - Meetings with sundry persons - Dorothy forges
ahead - Madame Pavlova spares Dublin

Though we lived at Foxrock we still attended the church at Carrick-mines where at one time we exercised almost full control of the choir. My mother's deafness prevented her from taking part in the music or indeed in following the service at all, so when it came to the time for the sermon she would produce her book of poetry, usually a large volume of Robert Browning, and sit reading it happily. The rector of our parish quite approved of this performance, but hoped the habit would not spread to the rest of the congregation.

Our rector was the Reverend George Newport Clark, a man of the gentlest, most Christian disposition. He lived with his wife, his mother-in-law, his sister-in-law, his brother-in-law and his one little daughter, Mary, a pretty, pert little girl who was the centre of his life. To us children she seemed the centre of the parish as well. She shared this position with a very large donkey named Reuben, who was owned by her Aunt Minnie. Minnie was as gentle and kindly a person as her brother-in-law. They were all ruled with a rod of iron by Mrs Clark and her mother, except Reuben who did what he liked and lived a life of laziness and luxury. Sometimes he allowed himself to be harnessed to a tiny phaeton and the whole family went for a drive, but most of his time was given up to being petted, adored and overfed by his devoted mistress.

Years and years later Katherine Mansfield wrote to me, 'Tell me more about Mary Clark.' There was really nothing to tell about Mary and I cannot remember ever having mentioned her to Katherine; but I must have done so, and she remembered the name and made it a sort of symbol for talks about our childhood.

My first serious proposal of marriage was from an elderly musical gentleman who came quite a distance to attend Carrickmines Church because 'the music was so good'. My mother was very upset when I told her that I had refused him. She said, 'He has four hundred pounds a year and a piano!' Her family had never been well-off and such riches to start married life on seemed enormous to her. My mother's one idea was to get her daughters married, but my romances never came to anything. The young men I preferred always seemed to be married to someone else.

Once, however, I really did get engaged. It was shortly after I joined the United Arts Club, which had its first premises in Lincoln Place. There was to be a club dinner. Hugh Lane arrived and, seeing the rather primitive furnishing and apparent poverty of our premises, in his princely way sent out for flowers for the table and champagne. At dinner a good-looking and attractive young architect, whom I had not met before, was opening a bottle of champagne; it was a very lively bottle and the contents went all over me. For all that, it was a delightful evening; I remember that I and some other young people spent most of it on the roof.

When the time came for me to catch the last train back from Harcourt Street to Foxrock, the young architect walked with me to the station. We met again next day and he asked me to marry him. I think he was rather taken aback when I accepted him and the match was not looked on with approval by his family. The engagement lasted several years; but the bogy of my father's shop terrified his people and finally frightened him away too.

By this time my appearance must have improved. Lady Gregory alludes to this dinner at the Arts Club in her biography of her nephew, Hugh Lane. She writes of me as 'the beautiful Miss E' and says that Hugh was very annoyed when I went on to the roof, I should have stayed below where Percy French was playing his banjo as I was 'part of the decoration of the room'.

Though our romances did not always run smoothly, Dorothy and I got great pleasure in other ways. We both belonged to the Orpheus Choral Society. There were about sixty of us altogether and we loved the rehearsals and our concerts with guest soloists. Dr Culwick was a great figure. How thrilled we were when he put his watch on his music-stand at a rehearsal and said, 'I must hear my watch ticking through your *pianissimo*.' We did not care much for the 'hey nonny-nonny' kind of madrigals but it was grand to sing the dramatic stuff: 'Dead in the Sierras' by Coleridge Taylor or 'The Dirge of Darthula' by Brahms.

It was Ida Elsner who had suggested that we two should go and have an audition. We arrived at Dr Culwick's house with our duet, 'Oh that we two were maying'. I am sure that we sang it charmingly—then he gave me a reading test which I got through somehow. Dorothy was very good at reading music. He gave her a piece to sing backwards and I could scarcely believe my ears when I heard her do it perfectly.

Dorothy and I were great devotees of the Moody-Manners Opera Company. We even thought of trying to get into the chorus and going on tour with the company. When we mentioned this idea to my father, he said with astonishment, 'You have a roof over your head, and plenty to eat. What more do you want?' It was too difficult to explain.

Though we were devoted to our father and grateful for his great care of his daughters, this sometimes became irksome to us. He used to ask us, 'Where were you?' or 'Who were you with?' It seemed so silly to have to explain that we had been having tea with some of our boy-friends in the Café Cairo in Grafton Street. Our behaviour was blameless and terribly innocent. After the late-night rehearsals of the Orpheus Choral Society he used to meet us at Foxrock Station to walk the ten minutes to our house with us. The thought of his two girls walking that distance alone in the dark was intolerable to him.

Father was grieved when we gave up going to church. He would appear on Sunday morning with his hat on his head and his waterproof over his arm and say, 'Well, girls, who is for church?' We would reply, 'You go, Papa, we have other ideas.'

Sarah Purser took me and another girl on a tour of the cathedrals and churches of England to study stained glass. The few memories I have of this tour, however, have nothing to do with windows. One relates to York Minster. We had been drawing all day, up in the clerestory and all over the place. It was getting late in the afternoon : time for evensong. I sat alone somewhere in the back of the vast cathedral, which at that time was lit only by candles.

After the service the organist went on playing, wandering from one thing to another. Then he began the Bach D Minor Toccata and Fugue. The whole place seemed to tremble and throb with the great volume of sound. It was as if something supernatural was happening in that most perfect setting—the great pillars of the nave soaring up into the darkness above, the few lights burning round the Communion table and choir-stalls. I came out almost intoxicated with emotion. I found my way back to the hotel and was surprised to find Sarah arriving at the same moment. She asked, 'Where have you been?' I told her. She simply said, 'I was there too.'

In the graveyard at Tewkesbury, the town where Sarah's ancestors had lived, we found tombstones with all the old family names on them—'Sarah Purser', 'John Purser', and so on. We inquired at the Post Office to find out whether any Pursers were still surviving in the place and were directed to the home of a very old man, who had been a stocking-maker.

As we entered the old man's cottage and saw him sitting by his fire, Sarah grasped my arm and said softly, 'It is John!' (John was her brother.) The likeness between him and her family was extraordinary. The old stocking-maker had a young woman looking after him; he was very deaf and Sarah had to shout at him. She told him that she too was a Purser, that her part of the family had gone to live in Ireland two hundred years before. He did not seem very interested and several times he pointed to me and asked, 'What relation is she to me?' He came out to his hall-door to be photographed, still insisting, much to Sarah's amusement, that I was the one he wished to be related to.

This trip finished in London, where some Irish M.P.s invited us to take tea on the terrace at the House of Commons. Sarah and her friends were talking politics when Mr Havilland Burke turned to me and said, 'Who would you like to see? Mention his name and we'll produce him.' I promptly said, 'Winston Churchill', at which they all laughed. They said that assignment would be too difficult.

Sarah Purser was rather impatient with illness; she never seemed to be ill herself. One spring she had to spend a couple of weeks in bed—I saw her when she had recovered and she said sadly, 'A terrible thing happened to me while I was ill.' I asked what it was, thinking she would tell me of a heavy fall in the value of her investments. She said, 'The copper-beech in front of the house came into leaf and I never saw it happening.'

My sister Edna had gone to live with a grandmother and aunt in Dublin, so Dorothy and I were now much together. We spent a lot of the time painting each other and anyone else we could get to sit. One year the subject for the Taylor Art Scholarship was 'Bedtime', and Dorothy wanted a small child to pose for her. Sam Beckett was just the right size and age. She took a photograph to work from of the future author of *Waiting for Godot* kneeling as if saying his prayers at his mother's knee.

The Becketts lived less than a mile from our house, and although Sam's mother was a much younger woman than mine they became great friends. This was largely due to the kindness of May Beckett's heart. She took pity on my mother because of her deafness. They were both interested in gardening, and I remember May Beckett coming flying on her bicycle with some new cutting or plant for my mother's garden. I know my mother valued her kindness and companionship very much.

After the sudden death of Walter Osborne in 1903, Dorothy gave up attending the painting school of the Royal Hibernian Academy, but she continued her painting at home and won the Taylor Scholarship several times. She also started to learn cooking and dressmaking, and then married a young South African doctor who had done his medical course in the College of Surgeons with Philip. She went to live in South Africa. I missed Dorothy mightily, for we had been close companions.

After Dorothy's departure one of my father's sisters very kindly gave me a sum of money. I had got very weary of stained glass so I decided to go to the Slade School in London and try to become a painter. The Dublin United Arts Club welcomed any excuse for a club dinner and my departure seemed to provide an excellent one. Many club members were expert ballad-writers. Among them was Susan Mitchell, the great friend and secretary of George Russell ('AE'). She used to make up topical rhymes and sing them for friends, and a number of them were afterwards reprinted in a small book called *Aids to the Immortality of Certain Persons in Ireland*.

George Moore was Susan's chief victim. In her collection are a series of cutting ballads entitled 'George Moore comes to Ireland', 'George Moore joins the Irish Church', 'George Moore becomes High Sheriff of Mayo', 'George Moore eats a Grey Mullet', 'George Moore becomes a Priest of Aphrodite'. Later she wrote a biography of him in the series *Irishmen of Today*. This nearly led to a breach between Moore and 'AE', since the former believed that the latter had had a hand in it or had at least sanctioned it.

Susan could be distinctly mischievous. She makes Moore say, in a rhyme written at about the time of the publication of *Ave*:

> My sins and my repentance all paper and all cram,
> Some day you'll all discover how respectable I am,
> How I revere the marriage state, believe in Abraham,
> And for Gaels and their revivals don't really care a damn.

It might not seem the most enviable experience to be hymned by such a sharp tongue, but Susan Mitchell relented in my case. Her little song about me was to the tune of 'She's over the border and awa' ', and it ran:

> Our pretty Beatrice departs
> To win her Art more grace,
> But she'll not fashion anything
> More lovely than her face.
> Apollo asks a sacrifice,
> With grief our hearts o'erflow.
> Oh, must we offer at his shrine
> The loveliest thing we know?

49

Arrived in London, I rented a small furnished flat in a women's hostel in Goodge Street. Orpen used to come to tea with me there and he loved to hear about all the goings-on at the Slade. He was still going to Ireland to teach in the School of Art, and would tell me of dinners in Jammet's with Oliver Gogarty, of Cissie and 'the Boss' and other of our friends. Also of parties at Howth; Orpen loved Howth. For several years he took a house on the south side of the hill, with its own bathing-place, and brought over his family to spend the summer there.

I was not much of a success at the Slade. Joseph Hone in his book on Tonks maintains that this great teacher was invariably kind to his pupils and an angel of consideration where the model was concerned. Actually, whether intentionally or not, he could be very crushing. In the life-class he stood before my easel and asked what I had been doing before I went there. I told him and he asked if I used living models for stained glass. I said 'No', that for years I had drawn and modelled from life, but for stained glass cartoons I just drew out of my head. Tonks said, 'I only know of one painter who did that.' I asked 'Who?' and he answered, 'Daniel Maclise.' I said, 'But no one wants to draw like Daniel Maclise.' He said, 'You do.'

When I moved into the painting-class, Steer sat in front of my easel and was silent for a long time; he looked at my name on the corner of my canvas and said, 'Tonks has spoken to me about you.' He did not tell me what Tonks had said. In fact the only other thing he said was, 'Well, carry on', which I found very disconcerting, as I thought I had done all that could possibly be done to that particular canvas, though the model had only started the pose that morning.

George Moore had gone back to live in London at about the time I went to the Slade. I met him in the street one day, and he stopped and said, 'Tonks has been speaking to me about you.' Again I was full of curiosity as to what he had said. I gathered it was something about my being 'too clever, too slick'.

George Moore asked me to dine with him and we went to the Café Royal. As he was helping me off with my coat, he said softly, 'Madam, may I undress you for the fight?' I capped it brightly with,

'The wars are naked which we make tonight.' He looked astonished, but I had just been reading Beaumont and Fletcher. We both laughed, but though I had been able to cap his quotation I was really very unsophisticated and innocent.

I remember how we talked about music at dinner and how Moore listened as if he was really interested and amused when I told him how I and my sisters had become keen Wagnerites at an early age, how we had learnt the vocal scores of some of the operas, how I sang all the tenor and bass parts and Dorothy the soprano and alto, and what fun we had dying together as Tristan and Isolde.

Like many young people Dorothy and I found great pleasure in tragic music. We had a piano arrangement for four hands of Tschaikovsky's *Symphonie Pathétique*, and we revelled in getting the last drop of despair out of the final movement, with its sinister drum-beat in the bass going on and on.

Another Dorothy—Dorothy Brett, later to become a friend of D. H. Lawrence and his wife Frieda—was also at the Slade at this time. I had noticed a tall girl with big brown eyes in the life-class who was slightly deaf. Tonks seemed to spend more time at her easel than with the rest of us. He evidently liked her. I asked one of the other girls who she was and she replied in an awed voice, 'The Honourable Dorothy Brett, daughter of Viscount Esher.'

It was years later, when I was living in London, in Selwood Terrace, that one night at the St John Hutchinsons' house I saw a tall girl whose appearance was familiar, but I could not place her. She was looking at me in a puzzled way; then she came across the room and said, 'Don't tell me.' After a little while we both remembered and exclaimed together, 'The Slade!'

Dorothy Brett went to Mexico with Lawrence and Frieda, and later she wrote a book about Lawrence which his friend Koteliansky disliked so much that when she came back to London on a visit and rang Kot up asking if she might come to see him, he said, 'No.' Afterwards he said that he approved the cheerful way in which she had replied, 'O.K.'

I never seemed to have any conversation with anyone at the

Slade School, except the very unsatisfactory kind that consists only of question and answer. One day there was some excitement going on over Gwen Darwin, who later wrote a most charming book, illustrated by herself, about her childhood in that great *Origin of Species* family. In reply to my inquiries I was told that she had just become engaged to Jacques Raverat, another Slade student, and that they had walked in from Oxford that morning to celebrate the occasion.

Before I left Dublin I had become friendly with a young man from Cambridge, Dominick Spring-Rice; and while I was at the Slade he took me to meet his mother, who lived in London. She was a very active suffragette. She thought that I should also work for 'the Cause'. She took me along to suffragette meetings and introduced me to some of the leaders. I admired the courage and determination of these women and even got as far as trying to sell the paper *Votes for Women* to people standing in theatre queues, but without much success. My heart was not in it. I was more interested in Dominick's efforts to educate me by lending me Restoration comedies and translations of Greek dramas.

While I was still at the Slade, my sister Dorothy wrote to me from South Africa to tell me that she was going to have a baby. This was a shock because I felt that she had passed by me and had gone ahead of me. Though she was younger than I was she had achieved something which was more worth while than what I was doing. Painting and drawing became very unimportant. Having a baby seemed the only possible satisfaction and fulfilment; but as there was not much that I could do about it, I had no choice but to continue with my 'Art Work'.

On my return to Ireland I spent a couple of weeks in Kerry with the Spring-Rice family and a young Cambridge friend of Dominick's, Frank Birch. This holiday remains in my memory as a time of enchantment. It was not only the young men; the very air of Kerry was steeped with beauty and mystery after Goodge Street, Gower Street and the Tottenham Court Road.

The last time Tonks had stood before my easel at the end of my short stay at the Slade he said, 'The speed, the slickness, the skill. It is *horrible*!' But back in Dublin again from Kerry, I took a room in Kildare Street as a studio, still hoping, in spite of Tonks's discouragement to become a painter.

It was about this time that Madame Anna Pavlova and a Russian ballet company came to Dublin. Orpen was also there and he got a box for the first night. Joseph Hone the writer and his wife Vera, whom Orpen had painted several times, came too. When we entered the theatre we were surprised to see an almost empty house; Dublin was just not interested in, or else completely ignorant of, ballet.

I had never seen ballet like this before. I was thrilled and excited; it seemed like visual, lovely, living music. We were all so moved that we leaned out of our box and applauded madly, especially after Pavlova died exquisitely as the Swan. When she came forward to bow she looked straight towards our box. Indeed, she treated us after every item as if we were her only audience, which we almost were.

Orpen noticed on the programme the name of a man he had met in former days in London (I think he was Pavlova's musical director). Orpen got in touch with this man and asked him to lunch next day in Jammet's. Vera and Joe Hone and I were also invited. We sat and waited at the table for Orpen's guest. He came in and said apologetically, 'Madame is downstairs and would like to join us.' Orpen and he hurried down and brought 'Madame' up.

Pavlova was exquisite. She wore a cloche hat which almost hid her little face and had a large bow in front made of some golden gossamer material. She spoke very little English, but with the aid of her interpreter she explained to us that, unlike the Lord in the Bible at the destruction of Sodom and Gomorrah, for the sake of *four* enthusiasts in the stage box she had decided to spare Dublin.

It was a pleasant lunch party. Orpen sent for some sheets of Jammet's writing-paper and made drawings of Pavlova, some of which he gave her. After lunch she said she had her own car waiting and would like to take us for a drive if we would show her Dublin. We drove round Phoenix Park. It was winter, the trees were bare and it looked desolate and dreary. We assured her it was the biggest park in the world except one in St Petersburg.

As the weeks went on, Dublin discovered ballet. On the last

53

night the house was packed with a wildly appreciative audience and Pavlova seemed to be very pleased with the city she had spared. Orpen had sent masses of flowers to be handed up to her, and a very large black bog-oak shillelagh, with a wide gold band around it, on which was inscribed, 'From the Four Roads of Ireland, and the Far-off Windy Hills', together with the date of her visit.

Some time after Pavlova's death in London, I was in the Print Room of the British Museum. I saw, hanging on the wall, one of the drawings which Orpen had made on Jammet's notepaper; she had presented it to the Museum. Behind her he had drawn the sentimental, rather comic mural of Spring, Summer, Autumn and Winter which was moved with the other murals when Jammet's took up its present abode in Nassau Street.

5

*A husband is found for me - I meet Katherine Mansfield
and Middleton Murry - A honeymoon and a home - Painters,
sculptors and literary lions in Paris - Kot and his friends*

Back home in Foxrock my father turned to me one day and said,
with an obviously assumed carelessness, 'Well, Bee, what about
finding a husband?' I felt that he and my mother had been worried
about me, getting so old (I was twenty-six) and not being married,
in spite of having had many admirers.

Cissie and 'the Boss' had a cottage on the Hill of Howth where
they lived with several small children and I went there to tell
them of this incident. They said, 'We have the perfect young man
for you.' He was Gordon Campbell, the eldest son of a distinguished
Dublin lawyer, and the poet Seamus O'Sullivan had brought him
out to Howth to meet them. Gordon Campbell had just discovered
the existence of music, painting and literature; things which were
almost unheard of in the Fitzwilliam Square society in which he
had grown up. To him, at that time, writers and artists seemed
very exciting and interesting people.

We met and were sufficiently pleased with each other to think
that getting married was a very sensible idea. Gordon had just
been called to the English Bar, which meant that we would go to
live in London. When his family heard of our plans the bogy of
my father's shop made one faint effort to put in an appearance,
but quickly faded away.

Before we were married in 1912, I went to London to look at a
little house in Selwood Terrace, South Kensington, which Gordon
was going to rent. While I was there he took me to meet two
friends of his who had a flat in Theobald's Road near Gray's
Inn. They were Katherine Mansfield and John Middleton
Murry.

When we arrived Katherine was sitting on a laundry basket at the top of the stairs, carrying on a gay conversation with a laundry-man in a high-pitched voice. She and Murry wore fishermen's navy blue jerseys and her hair was bobbed with a fringe across the forehead. Gordon had met Katherine at the house of the novelist W. L. George, who was a great admirer of hers. That night, when he had walked back to her flat with her, he had been impressed by her talk, the way 'she would stop every few yards and go into a poetic rhapsody about the beauty of the city'; he liked the happy unself-conscious way in which she engaged every night-watchman they passed in conversation. She invited him to tea one day to meet her lodger, John Middleton Murry.

Katherine and Murry thought a lot of Gordon. They had wonderful discussions with him about Dostoievsky which went on for hours. Katherine probably looked on me as a sort of interloper. That evening when we first met we all sat on the floor of her flat, for there was very little furniture. The conversation was about people going to bed with each other and other things that I had never heard mentioned in public before. I felt Katherine was trying to shock me and frighten me away. She was hard and bright and hostile. I never spoke a word.

There was another young man in Katherine's flat that evening, Frederick Goodyear, a strange and brilliant person, a scholar of Brasenose. He died of wounds in France in 1917. Goodyear had been at Oxford with Murry, and according to his tutors he was the ablest man who had come to the college in their time. He too was interested in writing and had a talent which might have developed into something very important if he had lived.

When we first met Katherine she had already published a book of short stories, *In a German Pension*. She had come to London as a young girl from New Zealand to study music, but it was not long before she decided that she wished to become a writer. With some idea of gaining 'experience', she got herself involved in about as much suffering as any young writer ever faced up to. A broken and meaningless marriage, unhappy love affairs, poverty, two pregnancies of illegitimate children of which one ended in a miscarriage and one in an abortion—through all this time one friend stood by her, a girl who had been with her at Queen's College, Harley Street.

This friend's name was Ida Baker, but she called herself 'Lesley Moore' because Katherine said that 'Ida Baker' was 'the ugliest name on earth'. For the rest of Katherine's life this girl remained most devoted to her, and in all Katherine's worst moments of illness or despair Ida Baker was with her, serving her and caring for her with what Koteliansky described as 'a unique form of love' During those tragic early years Katherine was steadily writing and gaining confidence in the art which meant everything to her.

I only once heard Katherine allude to her first husband, George Charles Bowden, while we were in Selwood Terrace. She had written to ask him to divorce her as she wanted to marry Murry. Bowden was in America on a concert tour—he was a singer. Katherine was very much amused when he wrote to her with pride saying that he was 'the only tenor on the coast'.

Gordon and I were married in August 1912. It was a very quiet wedding. Although Hugh Lane had said, 'You must be married in white, you must have a veil, you must have bridesmaids, a woman has only one day in her life, her wedding day', I was married in my everyday clothes. Then we went straight off to catch a train to Donegal, where we were to spend our honeymoon in Janie Stewart's farmhouse in Dunfanaghy, which had been recommended to us by George Russell ('AE') who used to spend his holidays there, painting.

It was the coldest August in the memory of man. At the end of the honeymoon we came back to stay with my people at Foxrock and saw an aeronautical display on Leopardstown Race Course. It was the first time that any of us had seen men flying. How we cheered and waved as the big, clumsy, kite-like machines zoomed over our heads, with the occupants bowing and waving back to us!

In October we went to live at No. 9, Selwood Terrace. It was then a rather shabby row of houses in a narrow street running from the Fulham Road into the upper-class and opulent Onslow Gardens. Since then, Onslow Gardens have lost their splendour and Selwood Terrace has become the opulent place, the home of film-stars, with yellow front-doors and shrubs in tubs.

At Christmas 1912 we went to Paris with Murry and Katherine. She had a painter friend there, Ann Estelle Rice, who had a large studio and was going to give a great Christmas party. Gilbert and Mary Cannan came too—Mary had been the wife of Sir James Barrie and had left him to marry Gilbert who had been his secretary. Gilbert Cannan was just beginning to be known as a novelist.

We were driving from the station to our hotel, somewhere near the Louvre, when I saw something that I had remembered and admired ever since my last visit to Paris. I could not help exclaiming, 'The Frémiet Joan of Arc!' There she sat on her little cob of a horse, in gilt bronze, so vitally alive and gay. Murry said to Katherine in his funny slow way, 'Tig, I told you she was all right.' They must have been discussing me. I was so grateful to Murry. I felt that Katherine accepted me after this incident. The name 'Tig' was an abbreviation of 'Tiger'—Katherine and Murry called themselves 'the Two Tigers'.

At that time in Paris, Katherine seemed very happy. I remember her gaiety, the way she would flounce into a restaurant and sweep her wide black hat from her bobbed head and hang it among the men's hats on the rack. I remember a group of men at a table running their tongues round their lips saying, 'Oh la la', and her little muted laugh, delighted with herself. She seemed to know a lot of painters there, or perhaps they were friends of Ann Rice's—Ferguson, Peploe, and a big woman who wore men's clothes and looked like Oscar Wilde and was always weeping. At night we went from café to café; there always seemed to be some terrific psychological drama going on, and we had to keep avoiding someone or other. A great discussion was also raging and it seemed to be eternally on the same subject: 'Was the *Titanic* a work of art?' The *Titanic* had been sunk on her maiden voyage to America in the spring of that year.

One night we were walking under some large arch-way, dimly lit; there was a stone seat running along the inside wall and on it, sitting and lying down, were a group of beggars in dark rags, dead still and silent. It was terribly queer and dramatic with a side-light from a street lamp. Katherine and I stopped to look, while the rest of the party went on. We spoke in whispers. There was no movement among the black, silent figures; they were terrifying, they had no faces. We hurried on after the others.

Through Katherine and Murry we got to know D. H. Lawrence and Frieda, Mark Gertler and S. S. Koteliansky, who became known to us all as 'Kot'. He had come to England about 1910 on a scholarship from Kiev University to do research work in economics. He said, 'I came for three months, and I stayed for ever.' His full name was Samuel Solomonovitch Koteliansky.

Kot's hair was black, and grew upwards in a strong, dark mass from his long, pale, sensitive face. He was of medium height, and his head was splendid and impressive. Leonard Woolf has written about him, 'If you know Kot well, you understand what a major Hebrew prophet must have been like. If Jeremiah had been born in a ghetto village of the Ukraine in 1880 he would have been Kot.'

Kot's childhood seemed to have been made up of a round of religious observances, pogroms and sufferings. In the village where he lived Yiddish was the only language spoken. At the age of nine years he told his parents that he no longer believed in the Jewish faith and he wished to learn Russian and go to a Russian school. This was a terrible blow to his family, but he got his way and finally went to the University at Kiev.

In Kiev, Kot had revolutionary sympathies. Katherine had a story about how he had organized a revolution there against the Czarist régime. On the day appointed for the rising, no one turned up at the meeting-place except Kot; he was so shattered that he started walking, and never stopped till he got to the Tottenham Court Road. He had a room there for some time after his arrival in London. To make himself look like an Englishman he bought a Panama hat and white tennis shoes; he also wore a Russian blouse with embroidered neckband. When he went out into the street the girls of Tottenham Court Road became so helpless with laughter that he used to stay in his room during the day and only come out at night.

Leonard Woolf writes of Kot's meeting with Lawrence on a walking tour in the Lake District in 1914, and of how they took to each other at once. 'Kot's passionate approval of what he thought good, particularly in people, his intense hatred of what he thought bad, the directness and vehemence of his speech, his inability to tell a lie—all this appealed strongly to Lawrence, and they became very fond of each other.'

Woolf goes on to tell of Kot's first meeting with Katherine. Kot had gone to stay for a weekend with Lawrence and Frieda in their cottage near Chesham. The Murrys also had a cottage close by. At lunch Frieda began lamenting about how much she missed her children (she had left her husband and family in order to marry Lawrence) and Kot said, 'Frieda, you must choose either your children or Lawrence. If you choose Lawrence, you must stop complaining about the children.'

After lunch Frieda left them and Lawrence and Kot sat talking while the rain poured down in torrents. Suddenly the door opened and there stood a young woman in Wellington boots, with her skirts tucked up, soaking wet, who said, 'Lorenzo, Frieda has asked me to come and tell you that she will not come back.' 'Damn the woman,' shouted Lawrence in a fury. 'Tell her I never want to see her again.' The young woman said nothing, but turned and went out into the rain. It was Katherine Mansfield and this was the first time that Kot saw her. Later they became great friends, and Katherine's feeling for Kot is clearly shown in her letters and journals. He was the only person whom she trusted and respected completely, and of Katherine, Kot always said, 'She is a real person.'

About Kot's work as a translator, Leonard Woolf has written: 'Kot was a fine translator from the Russian, and at one time or another Lawrence, Katherine Mansfield, Virginia Woolf and I collaborated with him in translating books by Tolstoy, Dostoevski, Tchekhov, Gorky, and Bunin. The translation of Bunin's *Gentleman from San Francisco*, which he did with Lawrence, is magnificent, and Gorky's *Reminiscences of Tolstoy* is a very remarkable book. His method was to write out the translation in his own strange English and leave a large space between the lines in which

I then turned his English into my English—after I had turned his first draft into English English, we then went through it sentence by sentence. Kot had a most sensitive understanding of and feeling for language and literature and also a strong and subtle mind. He would pass no sentence until he was absolutely convinced that it gave the exact shade of meaning and feeling of the original and we would sometimes be a quarter of an hour arguing over a single word. Yes, Kot was "a real person".'

I do not remember my first meeting with Kot, but he said his first memory of me was when I opened the hall-door of No. 9, Selwood Terrace to him. 'I thought you had a nice face,' he told me later.

Kot shared Lawrence's habit of denunciation, but he had a greater gift for friendship than Lawrence had. I think this group of people first came to our house drawn by Gordon's talk and Gordon's mind. They found it a homely place and liked being there; they were all rather homeless people. For one reason or another Katherine and Murry, Lawrence and Frieda were always moving about, making little nests and leaving them again to go somewhere else.

Murry had gone up to Brasenose College, Oxford, with a scholarship from the Blue Coat School. His keen, analytical mind and his aptitude for literature had marked him out as a student of exceptional ability. He met Katherine at a time when he had lost interest in Oxford and did not even want to sit for his Schools. Katherine persuaded him to leave college, whereupon they decided to share her flat and began to work together on a magazine which he and an Oxford friend had founded—the magazine was called *Rhythm*.

Murry, with his handsome face and beautiful eyes, had an appealing charm, as if he were saying, 'I am really only a little boy, be good to me.' This quality probably meant much to Katherine, but she needed even more the quality of what she called a 'Pa-Man', someone to lean on, someone to look up to, who would bear all the burdens and be cheerful and brave in every circumstance. She must often have found Murry a broken reed. Murry used to say that Katherine and I 'romanticized' Kot, making him a tower of strength, a moral genius incapable of saying or doing a dishonourable thing. Perhaps this was partly true. I think I held to this view of Kot long after she began to waver, but to the end of her life she turned to him and valued him as a very rare and faithful friend.

6

Gordon and Murry with rucksacks on their backs went away for
a few days to walk in the country while Katherine came to stay
with me.

The friendship which was growing up between them was very
important to them both. For Gordon the long talks with Murry
were an exciting intellectual experience, something which he had
not yet known, full of possibilities of revelation and illumination
on all sorts of profound subjects. Gordon was not interested in
Murry's humanity or his personal life. The whole relationship was
enveloped in a sort of innocence which at the present time might
be difficult to understand. I think that Murry needed something
more emotional and dramatic than the purely intellectual fare
that Gordon delighted in. It was as if he was looking for a Messiah
and had decided on Gordon to fill that role for him.

In the following letter, dated 1 February, 1915, Murry writes of
how Gordon 'failed him'.

Dear Gordon,

I've been wondering whether I wd. write to you or not. (Even
now I wonder whether I'll post this, and if I'll manage to say
what I want to say.)

You may—or may not—have found me strange on the evening when we left London. At all events whether you felt it or
not, I was. I had gone through a couple of bad days.

It's a curious thing for a person like me when he comes to
the knowledge that he is absolutely alone. That's what had

happened. It took me four days to realise it, one day to feel it, and God knows how long it will take me to get over it. A kind of desolation is hanging about me now as I write—something deadening that though I grope at it with my two hands I cannot get away. I don't see the sun anymore through the clouds.

The funny thing is that you won't believe this is all to do with you. I believe that in some way you know it, for all that, or rather I can't believe that you don't know it. I can't believe that I made such a bloody mistake as all that. What is funnier is that I can look at it all from your side and see that it is all a trivial kind of happening. Why in God's name should it have been important that I was waiting for you to come here on Saturday week, that I rode into Chesham miserable after your telegram came, that I made myself cheerful again coming back with the thought that you would come after all, that I tried to work in the evening, and when I heard a cart stop outside, my heart stopped too, stopped so that I could hardly breathe for a long while—it all seems silly as I write it—were it not that I went through it.

Well, as I say, it took me four days to make up my mind that I can't go through that again—for nothing. It took me all that while to make up my mind that you had failed me. (I speak only from my side. Don't think there's any accusation, at all.) It is as though I had held fast by you for long—I have known you all the living time of my life—and when I began to bear upon you, you bent under the weight—as though I stretched to find the inmost of you and found an emptiness. I must have needed you badly then. Now, I can't judge your book, because I grope in the same emptiness, so that I could cry. If anyone cried without tears, I did that night you read it to me. And now I think of the ridiculous way I tried not to come and see you then, to prove to myself that I was strong enough not to need you. I don't know, but I think I could have stayed away for myself; but I couldn't bear to fail you. Perhaps, I think now, had I been staying with you when we were in London, I might have got back to the old state—but destiny has its own ways. I knew certainly that there is destiny when, after hurrying with my mind finally made up

S. S. Koteliansky and Katherine Mansfield, 1916, at 24 Norfolk Road, London

Middleton Murry, Frieda Lawrence, D. H. Lawrence, 9 Selwood Terrace, London

Beatrice Glenavy, 1925

Biddy and Michael, Arosa, 1938

Gordon Campbell with Paddy and
Biddy, Greystones, 1919

to state the whole thing on meeting you, your voice sounded over the telephone to say it was impossible.

It seems to me now that I asked too much of you—but then, I wonder, can I ask *too* much—I of you. Not the I that I was or the you I imagined. There was some stupid mistake—some romantic imagination of my own, it may have been. Whatever it was, it was a good thing, for now I can see that I must have loved you as one man seldom loves another. I look back at myself and find that I would have given you anything. I had very little to give, I know, but all that I did give you, or tried to give.

(All the while I am writing, I stop, to see whether I am exaggerating, being sentimental. I don't know. It may be. I can't see these things plainly now.)

Then I feel I am writing to two persons in you :—one that loved me, one that will say—what the hell's happened because I couldn't come down for a weekend. There's no need to answer, but if you do, don't let the second you answer; it would hurt me, and I find I have an amazing capacity for being hurt. I can't get on straightforwardly with this. I seem to see it so differently every moment, or rather a different angle of it hurts me.

I say to myself sometimes that perhaps this is all imagination, that it is really all as your second self would see it. I can't believe it. Somehow I know that you must have known.

I can't throw myself into an abyss. I have to gather myself together now and have the courage of my loneliness. It will be an effort for me to keep away from you. I don't delude myself about that. I'm not one of the strong men. Besides my love for you grew quietly and in secret. I never knew that it was there until it snapped, at about 8 o'clock of the night of last Saturday week, if you would know. It took two years. I can't get rid of it in a day. I have to screw myself up against you, now, and go my own way. At moments I thought I hated you for it—but it wasn't true. We might have pulled off some great thing to-gether; but you were divided—perhaps I was divided too. Perhaps we came together too late.

There's a line of finality about all this, I know—as though I should never see you again. We probably shall see each other often. We shall always be good friends if only for the people we despise together—but that doesn't mean very much—not to me, now.

I can hear Lawrence say that it would only have been possible between a man and a woman. I don't think so. It was possible for us, had you been other than you are. But you were and are yourself, and then it was not only impossible, but beyond a certain point not valuable for you. Perhaps it wasn't valuable for me. At present I feel too much hurt by life to get to that point of view. I seem to have served up too much of my naked soul to the world—it has always been trodden on, but this was the most unkindest cut of all.

J.M.M.

The letter was not posted until thirty-seven years later, when Murry had become a farmer in Thelnetham. In writing to Murry in 1952 Gordon said that he found it odd that Murry should have taken to farming; he received this reply:

Your remark about the oddity of J.M.M. of 1914 finishing up in this way—and it *is* damned odd—made me hunt out this letter I wrote to you in 1915. It suddenly turned up 2 or 3 years ago when I was gathering together my letters to Katherine. I'm glad to think I had the saving grace *not* to send it—and yet to keep it.

It's strange, not to be able to re-live the past. There's something in this letter which is quite mysterious to me. I only remember the shock, and the sort of numbness, and the utter unexpectedness of it: at the time it seemed the most awful thing that had ever happened to me, and the most awful thing that ever could happen. I was to be taught better, with a great deal of care on the part of the Almighty. But it was pretty grim.

And I suppose you were right—much wiser than I. But you will believe me, Gordon, when I say that I was utterly innocent and naive; and that I have always cherished the memory of my great affection for you. No man ever came near to taking the place you had in my heart.

And that's why I am truly glad to have seen you again, and to know that something has endured 'in spite of all'—that was Katherine's phrase. It means (in her language) that of love nothing is lost—not really. And that is my conviction—the only religious belief I have. It covers the lot, if only the truth were known. I have a hunch that is what you also believe.

There is no record of Gordon's reaction to Murry's strange letter, but he evidently thought that it was of value to Murry as he offered to send it back. For Murray wrote:

No, I don't want the letter back. I copied it before I sent it you, just as a document. I found it interesting, and strange. How *could* you have had any idea what was happening in me? (I ask myself now), and yet I seem to have taken it for granted that you had. All very odd. Most surprisingly, I find traces of much the same thing happening to Swift at about the same age —to Swift of all people, one would say. But I don't think I'm mistaken. It seems, indeed, that it took a couple of personal crises—one with a man, the other with a woman—to fashion the Swift of the books and the legend.

As for me, it took me a long while to feel any secure sense of my own identity. For years and years, I seemed to myself a sort of hollow shell—vastly sensitive, but uttterly empty : a real nothingness inside. (The only man I've read about who seems to have had, for years, precisely *this* experience is Coleridge.) So personal relations were all-important to me. They gave me a (very precious) assurance that there was a J.M.M., and at the same time I was incapable of a genuine personal relation. For I think the *sine qua non* of a personal relation is the secure possession of one's own identity—to be able to say surely 'I am I'— no matter what a poor thing it may be. So I was caught in a really vicious circle.

The reason why my affection for you took the extravagant

turn it did, I am pretty sure, is that Katherine, at that time, was withdrawing from me, and preparing to leave me: for the very sound reason, that there was no Murry. And when I knew that was happening, I clung desperately in my mind to the idea of you. (So much is pretty plain to me. Indeed, comparing the dates, I find that at the moment I wrote that letter she had actually gone off—to Paris. If she had stayed away, I might perhaps have faced my own nothingness and become a something. But that didn't happen until she died—and for that reason.)

While our two young men were away Katherine and I sat at the fire darning our husbands' socks and talking of our homes and childhood. We conjured up the excitement of the day of a party: the preparations, washing our hair and plaiting it to make it wavy, putting 'baby' ribbon in our camisoles; the wonderful feeling of pleasurable anticipation while waiting till the last moment to put on the party dress; then the hooking-up, the few stitches, and the running from room to room to look in the glass; the nice faint smell of the long white kid gloves, the white silk stockings and satin slippers.

Some time later Mary Cannan was talking about Katherine, saying she was 'so remote, and reserved, unapproachable, impossible'. I said I did not find her so, and told Mary about our talks. Mary laughed and said, 'Oh yes, Katherine always gives everyone what they want.'

Katherine was a very difficult person to know. Behind her little expressionless mask of a face an endless turmoil of emotion and thought seemed to be going on. She was very complex, also very self-critical and self-centred, struggling to make herself different, to get rid of what she considered the bad parts of herself. She was terribly private, and sometimes hard to approach; she could be so false and unreal that you shrank from her. This was probably a sort of armour, something to protect her intense hypersensitiveness. At other times she could be warm and gay and sympathetic, with what Dominick Spring-Rice described as 'a delicate taste in bawdy'. In these moods it was great happiness to be with her. Her courage was enormous, and so was her capacity to make fun of her sufferings, her illnesses, and her poverty.

Kot used to say that when Murry published her letters and diaries after her death he 'left out all the jokes', to make her an 'English Tchekov'. Beside her, I used to feel so simple, almost a simpleton. I think she found it easy to be with me; we had something in common when we first met, a memory of childhood in a distant provincial setting in another land. It was rather as if we were both exiles and did not quite 'belong' in London, but we both loved being alive in this wonderful, beautiful, tortuous and often torturing world.

While Katherine and Murry were living near us in Selwood Terrace we went round one evening to see them. As we approached their house we met Murry running towards us, looking wild and distracted, his hair flying. He said Katherine had suddenly been taken ill and he was going for a doctor, so Gordon went with him while I hurried on to Katherine. I found her seated in a chair, gasping for breath. She seemed to have lost her voice. She was wearing a new bright-yellow cardigan of knitted silk—in those days it was called a 'golf coat' and had just become fashionable. She was clutching the sides of the coat and saying in a fierce whisper, 'The death jacket, the death jacket!' I thought she was delirious and tried to calm her; she kept on gasping and trying to speak.

In spite of her agony she was trying to tell me a story in connection with the heart-attack, or whatever her sudden illness was. A little later Gordon and Murry returned with a very odd-looking doctor; he prescribed some brandy, took his fee and left. When Katherine had recovered she told us how the wife of W. L. George, the novelist, had been very ill somewhere in the country. W. L. George, who was in London, suddenly felt very sorry for her; he bought the coat and took a taxi and went to her. According to Katherine, 'She put the coat on and died.' W. L. George, horrified at the waste of money, tore it off her, got into another taxi, dashed back to London and gave the coat to Katherine. When he had gone she put the coat on and immediately had a heart-attack.

Some time later Katherine had the coat dyed a dark wine colour 'to take the harm out of it'. She had few clothes and felt that she must make use of such an expensive garment.

Sometimes Katherine used to 'put on acts', what Gertler called 'doing her stunts'. One evening in a basement sitting-room in Selwood Terrace she wept and threw herself about wailing, 'I am a soiled woman.' No one but me seemed impressed by her performance. I never knew at the time how much she was putting it on or suspected she might really be rather enjoying herself.

One of her most dramatic scenes took place during the Christmas we spent in Paris in 1912, when we had gone to see Ann Rice's paintings at her studio. A chair was suitably placed for Katherine, while Ann Rice, warm-hearted and generous, put canvases on the easel, and after a few minutes removed them and put others in their place. Perhaps Katherine started with too much enthusiasm and appreciation. This was understandable, as Ann Rice was a very good painter. After about a dozen pictures had been put on the easel Katherine began to wilt and become silent. Suddenly, to the astonishment of us all, she burst into floods of tears and heart-broken sobs. Ann Rice was terribly upset and there was general consternation. Katherine was led away gasping, 'The colour, the form, the light—it is all just as I feel it myself.' We left the studio carrying a picture presented to Katherine by Ann, as some compensation for causing her so much distress. Katherine laughed at the whole business afterwards.

There was a time when Katherine talked about going to live in one of the Southern States of the U.S.A. She wanted a 'coal-black Mammy'; life without such a thing seemed impossible. She made all sorts of plans, and then the subject was dropped. I had taken it all seriously, and eventually I asked when she and Murry were going. Katherine said, 'That is all finished. We have been there.' I asked about the coal-black Mammy. She replied, 'I have finished with her too.'

At one time the Murrys had a cottage at Cholesbury, near Chesham, which Gordon was supposed to share with them for weekends. I only went there once, and the visit was not a success.

The weather was cold and showery, and Katherine had been ill. She had asked us to bring some meat, but we forgot about it on our way to the station. However, when we arrived at Cholesbury we found a butcher, who apparently only sold legs of mutton, procured one and went on to the cottage where Katherine and I cooked it for an early dinner. It was not very tasty but we ate it, and she and I then proceeded to wash up.

Gordon and Murry went out into the little back-garden to make a paved path to the outdoor sanitation, 'so that Katherine would not get her feet wet on the muddy track'. They dug a shallow trench along the centre of the path and placed large stones in it which made a very uneven and treacherous sort of causeway. The man who owned the cottage lived near by and, noticing them working in the garden, came over to see what they were at. He was furious, and told them to restore the path to its former state. They did so, and came back to the cottage looking rather crest-fallen, to find an even worse state of affairs there.

The grease from the leg of mutton had completely defeated us in the washing-up operations. We had very little hot water and no washing-powder, and the grease was in thick layers over every-thing. Even the outlet to the sink was blocked with it and it was quite impossible to get it off the knives and forks. I tried to make a joke of our predicament but Katherine was beyond jokes; she started to weep ceaselessly and hopelessly. I felt there must be some deeper reason for her tears than the grease, and this idea was reinforced when she suddenly cried out in her distress, 'I want lights, music, people!' Even if 'lights, music, people' had suddenly appeared, I doubt whether she would have been comforted.

I remember myself as being in those days rather silent and in the background during the great talks. Before I went to the Slade I was part of a circle, a clique, a coterie centred on the Arts Club in Dublin. My departure to London had been treated as a sort of minor national disaster, which was all very flattering and pleasant. At the Slade School I was very much alone, a nobody—which I also found quite pleasant, enjoying just looking on. On my second departure to London, after I was married, I again found myself of no account, a looker-on. I hardly spoke. I made the tea.

71

One day Kot said to me, 'Believe in yourself, do not be afraid.' I was astonished, I had not thought that I was afraid or that I did not believe in myself. I just felt that the people I now knew who gathered round Gordon were different, more important than anyone I had met before. One evening they were all discussing 'magic' in poetry, and quoting lines from different poems in search of the magical phrase, Kot's advice gave me courage to speak. I said, 'What about William Morris's "Over the tender bow'd locks of the corn"?' Murry said, 'She has got something there, she is right.' I was very pleased, and grateful to Murry for being my champion, as he had been once before, in connection with the Frémiet statue. I probably became more aggressive from then on.

I enjoyed having a little house of my own and spent a lot of time trying to make it look agreeable. It was impossible to get anything to grow in the small garden at the back; the stuff you had to plant things in did not seem to be clay at all. I finally abandoned it to the cats of the neighbourhood, who in any case seemed to think it was their private property. I had to teach myself something about cooking and housekeeping. The School of Art and the Stained Glass Works had not been much help in instructing me in the art of buying meat and keeping accounts.

We had a mixed collection of daily helps, none of whom lasted very long. One young girl arrived one day with a tin of petrol; she said her chauffeur boy-friend had given it to her to wash her hair with, and she had no idea that it was dangerous or inflammable. If I had not stopped her in time she would have put it on her hair and proceeded to dry it at the fire. Then there was an old woman who drank, and terrified me by 'passing out' in the kitchen. We had one treasure, however—Mrs Conybear—who became well known to everyone who came to the house. (Lawrence has written of her in some of his letters.) She had an enormous cat which she brought with her every day, a cat fed on cods' heads— the smell of the cods' heads cooking sometimes made life in our little house almost unbearable.

In the spring of 1913 I went to Dublin, so that Patrick Campbell should be born in Ireland. After his arrival I stayed on with my family in Foxrock till Gordon came over for his vacation at the beginning of August. We had taken a cottage on the Hill of Howth where we went with the baby and a nurse, and Katherine and Murry joined us later. I had always had a passion for babies, but I do not think this enthusiasm was shared by Katherine, though she watched with interest any activities concerning the child. He figured a couple of years later in one of her short stories as a small boy riding on a leopard-skin on the back of a sofa.

Cissie and 'the Boss' lived in a much larger cottage some distance away from ours, and kept open house for all the poets, writers and painters of Dublin; indeed, for all the freaks and oddities as well. A sort of permanent party seemed to be going on there, with endless talk and drink and intermittent music and dancing. It was lively, warm and human, with children tumbling all over the place.

We used to bathe together on a beach at the foot of the cliff. One morning I saw a young woman clambering over the rocks, some distance away, and coming towards us. Katherine said, 'It is Ida Baker. I am going to her. Don't let the others follow me.' I was most surprised as I did not know that Ida was in Ireland. I had met her in London and Katherine had told me of their friendship, and of Ida's devotion to her, and how at times Katherine treated her very badly but 'could not live without her'. I suggested that Ida should join us—'We'd love to have her, we can get a bed, etc.'—but Katherine said that Ida would hate that; she was staying in some little hotel in the village of Howth. She had come to Ireland to be near Katherine and if they could be together for a short time every day, she would be happy.

I watched Katherine go to her, and the two figures sat on a rock and talked earnestly for some time. I had a feeling that Katherine was telling her how much she disliked being in Howth; the people, the noisy children, the idleness, the simple pleasures that Murry seemed to be enjoying so much—pottering round the fishing-boats in the harbour or going out in a sailing-boat. When the two figures had finished their talk Ida clambered over the rocks and disappeared into the distance. We did not see her again nor did Katherine mention her.

We had set off one day to sail to Ireland's Eye. It was fairly rough with a stiff breeze. Katherine was in misery, crouching at the bottom of the boat and wailing to be put on dry land. I felt just as terrible, but Gordon, Murry and the rest of the party were enjoying it immensely.

I think Katherine was enduring Howth for Murry's sake. I fear that lovely bay and its beautiful line of hills on the far side, its masses of gorse with that wonderful heavy warm perfume, meant nothing to her at that time. The life seething in her mind, and her longing to write, were completely absorbing her.

Katherine and I used to walk to the village of Howth to do shopping. One evening, on our way back, we saw Murry and Gordon standing on a little hill, silhouetted against the sky. Some trick of light made them look larger than life-size, as Katherine said, 'like Gods.' They stood with bowed heads, engrossed in something they were making, and we hurried forward, full of curiosity to see what they were at. They were tying little bundles of paper and grass on to a long bit of string, making a tail for a kite.

There was a natural bathing-pool in the rocks where we used to bathe. Once a full tide swept a shoal of herring fry into this pool. We caught them (with great difficulty and much laughter) in a bathing-towel, stumbling and staggering about in the water, the fry escaping only to be surrounded and caught again. We carried our catch back to the cottage and fried and ate them. I think Murry was sorry to leave Howth, the fishing and the kite-flying, but I felt that Katherine was not happy there and was glad when the time came for them to return to London.

In October of that year we returned to our nice little house in London, to Mrs Conybear and the cat. While we had been away Kot and Gertler had become friends, and they came together to Selwood Terrace. I was very interested to meet Gertler, whose work I had seen at the New English Art Club Exhibitions, and whose reputation at the Slade School had created as much excitement as that of Orpen and Augustus John.

Mark Gertler was born in London, at Spitalfields, in 1891. His parents were of Jewish-Austrian origin. At fourteen he worked in a stained glass window factory in Bloomsbury. Then a Jewish organization, the Educational Aid Society, which helps its coreligionists in the East End, sent him to the Slade, and he was quickly recognized as a serious and important painter.

When he was a boy in Whitechapel, Wertheimer 'took him up'. He was to be sent to Italy to study art and great things were to be done for him. There was tremendous excitement among his people when Wertheimer's Rolls-Royce arrived with a chauffeur and a footman to take him and his painting to Wertheimer's house to be inspected. As he was putting his canvases in the back of the car, the footman leaned forward and said, 'Be careful of the paint.' Gertler replied gaily, 'It's all right, they are quite dry.' The footman said, 'The paint on the car.' Gertler later decided not to be 'taken up' or sent anywhere, a decision which distressed his family.

Gertler was good-looking but his charm was the opposite of Murry's. He seemed always to be saying, 'Don't touch me. Leave me alone.' He was just as much in need of sympathy and under-standing as Murry, but unable to ask for it. It was his fierce in-dependence that endeared him to Kot, who was older than he was by about ten years and almost looked on him as his own son.

When we first knew Kot he was living in a place in Whitechapel called the Russian Law Bureau. There was another lawyer there who was his boss. He was known as 'the Black Beard'. I once went there with Katherine and Murry and she was delighted with the hideousness of it all: the darkness, the horsehair-covered furni-ture, a picture of kittens playing in a basket of pansies, and an even more incongruous picture for such a place, a Christ surroun-ded by little children. Talking to Gertler about it afterwards, we wondered what Kot did there as there must have been very little demand for Russian law in London. Gertler said, 'Kot's job is to black his boss's beard.'

Unfortunately, the Irish nanny whom we had brought to London with us suffered very much from homesickness, especially on one evening every week, when a man played 'It's a long way to Tipperary' on a cornet in our street. If it was pouring with rain or there was a thick fog this tune seemed very moving. It was then a completely new tune to me. Little did we think that this was to become the theme-song, the marching-song, of an army in a World War!

75

The nanny also complained of being very lonely; so I showed her the way to Kensington Gardens and she went there pushing the pram. I thought she might make friends with some of the other nannies, but she said they were 'terrible grand' and she preferred to 'keep herself to herself'.

7

*My family is increased and war begins - I have a distraught
visitor - Sunday evenings in St John's Wood - Gertler
entertains - Expeditions with Katherine Mansfield - At Lady
Ottoline's - Kot comforts - Katherine Mansfield has romantic interludes - A visit to Acacia Road - The toll of war*

In the early summer of 1914 I again went to Dublin, taking the
nurse and my small boy with me. I left them with my in-laws and
went into a nursing-home for the birth of my baby girl 'Biddy'.
One day while I was in the nursing-home I heard the newspaper
boys shouting 'Stop Press', telling of the murder of the Archduke
Ferdinand and his wife at Sarajevo. I had known that world affairs
were somehow at boiling-point, but it was all so complicated, so
very far away and so difficult to understand, that I had paid little
attention; besides, I was now completely wrapped up in the happiness of having two children.

The children and I and a new nanny were at my father's house
at Foxrock when war was declared. I remember sitting on the
lawn in the sunshine having tea. Two boy-friends of Marjorie's
were there, talking excitedly about how to obtain commissions in
the Army and get drafted to the Front before the war was over.
They just could not get into the Army quickly enough, they were
so afraid they might be missing something. The air seemed full of
a sense of adventure and the general impression was that the war
could hardly last till after Christmas.

The new nanny, Alice, was a grand person. Young and good-
looking, she came from Tipperary and was one of a very large
family. She lived with us for years and ruled the house and everyone in it.

We had a cottage in Howth that summer, and she and I and the
children stayed on there, because of the war, after Gordon had
gone back to London. From our cottage we had a wonderful view
of Dublin Bay filled with troop-ships lying at anchor. Men were

being called up, regiments mobilized all over the country. One morning when we got up all the ships had vanished, having slipped away silently into the night with their cargoes of men to 'unknown destinations'.

As nothing very terrible seemed to be happening in London we went over there to join Gordon in the late autumn. Frieda and Lawrence had stayed with Gordon in Selwood Terrace while we were away. By now Frieda had left her English professor husband and her three children, the divorce proceedings were over, and she and Lawrence had just been married.

I did not meet either of them until one day, in answer to a knocking on the front door, I opened it and saw a woman standing there dripping with rain and tears, her face blotched and red with weeping. She had a wide straw hat on which hung down all round her face, shapeless with water, and her hair was wet and straggling; she looked quite mad. She must have seen the blank look on my face, for I was just going to shut the door when she wailed, 'Don't you know me? I am Frieda.' I took her in and dried her while she told me, with more tears, how she had been standing behind a hedge near her old home waiting to see her children return from school. The rain had poured down on her; she had no umbrella. When at last the children appeared and went into the house she was so blind with weeping that she could hardly see them.

While we were in Ireland, Gordon had found a new house for us in St John's Wood, as the little house in South Kensington had now become too small. We moved into our new home the year after Gordon began to work in the Ministry of Munitions. It was charming, with a pear tree and an almond tree in the back-garden. Some time after we had settled there Murry and Katherine took an equally charming little house in Acacia Road, about five minutes' walk from ours. Kot and Gertler and the Murrys used to come to us on Sunday evenings. Life would have been very pleasant if it had not been for the growing horror of the war in the background.

Gertler was a great source of entertainment to us with his wonderful story-telling. He loved to act his stories, imitating everyone.

He described a party at the Russian Ballet (then the rage of London) when everyone went round Lopokova's dressing-room after the show. Gertler would go out of the room and return as Lady Ottoline Morrell, then as one of the Stracheys or Sitwells or Maynard Keynes or some other, making himself fat or tall, short or thin, while we all laughed helplessly. Kot's laugh was like a small continuous cough. In those days he wore pince-nez, and he had to take them off to wipe the tears of laughter from his eyes.

Gertler's appetite for parties was insatiable. He worked very hard during the day but seemed incapable of resting when he had finished painting. Socially he was a great success, for he seemed to know everyone and was invited everywhere. He loved music-halls and would give imitations of the turns that he saw there. He called himself and Kot 'Beattie and Babs' after two famous music-hall sisters who did a comic turn together.

The children's nurse, Alice, used to say that I went 'hat-mad' in the spring. Katherine sometimes shared this madness with me. We took our hats to pieces and tried to remould them nearer to our heart's desire. We also worked on our blouses, cutting off the sleeves, putting frills round the necks, but somehow they never became the lovely garments we intended.

Katherine and I sometimes went shopping together. One day in some big store she tried on about a dozen blouses; it went on for so long that she finally became exhausted, so did the shop-assistant. There was always something wrong with the pattern, the fit or the material. Suddenly I heard her make a decision and give a completely fictitious name and address for it to be sent to, saying it would be paid for on delivery. Out in the street again we were both shocked at what she had done. She said, 'I couldn't think of any other way of getting out of that shop. We might have been there for ever.'

Someone told Katherine about the ambulance trains arriving at Charing Cross Station; she wanted to go there, and I went with her. We stood among the waiting crowds, where people bought flowers and cigarettes. There was a great air of excitement, with Red Cross officials hurrying about. When the train came in the bad cases were carried out and put into closed ambulances. The

79

walking wounded seemed very cheerful, and were singing and cheering; they were put into large lorries and people ran after them throwing them flowers and cigarettes. Katherine did so too. We saw a flower-girl at the station gates gather all the flowers out of her baskets and run after a lorry and throw them in a shower on top of one man.

I remember another occasion when a party of us went at a rather late hour to Lady Ottoline Morrell's house. It was the first time I had met her. Lawrence was in a particularly fierce mood, accusing Gordon of being 'the devil behind the Cross' and of having 'a legal mind'. Gordon was fighting back. There was another Russian there besides Kot, and they were both being very angry with each other in Russian. Murry and Gertler were silent. Ottoline was hardly allowed to speak at all.

Katherine and I found ourselves wandering round the large drawing-room examining pictures and furniture, and she said softly to me, 'Do you feel that we are two prostitutes and that this is the first time we have ever been in a decent house?' I knew she was acting a part and wanted me to join in the game. It had been raining on our way there and we were rather damp and bedraggled, which helped the illusion.

Though Lady Ottoline was treated rather as a joke by Gertler and the other young people, in reality they were all rather in awe of her. She was half-sister to the Duke of Portland, and Philip Morrell, her husband, was a Liberal Member of Parliament. She was a unique personality, behind whose oddness and eccentricity there was a great and gracious lady. Gertler used to give very funny imitations of the way she spoke, a sort of cooing, moaning noise. In appearance Lady Ottoline was almost bizarre, with her height, her wild mahogany-coloured hair and her very personal style of dress. She was a generous and good friend to all those young people, and did not always receive the gratitude which she rightly deserved.

There were times when Katherine was ill and Murry was not much help to her. In fact, he seemed to collapse and crumple up, looking pale and distracted. I remember Katherine turning on him at such a time and saying, 'Must *you* look so ill?' Kot was always a great help and comfort to her. Before she went away on one of her journeys she said to me, 'I leave you a comforter.' When I asked, 'Who?' she replied 'Kot.'

I once talked with Gertler about Kot as a 'comforter', and found he too had had experience of Kot in that role. We agreed that Kot's way of comforting was to say, 'There is no comfort, you must face it.' But such a wealth of sympathy and understanding seemed to breathe out from him that it amounted to comfort in the end.

Katherine once told me about an incident in a train in France, during the war. The train was travelling in darkness because of the black-out, and she was feeling frightened and alone, when a sailor from the French Fleet got into her carriage and sat beside her. Without speaking he took her hand and held it; he played with it, slipping off her ring and putting it on different fingers, very gently, while she pretended to be asleep. He got out at some station without making any sign of recognition of their fleeting relationship, and when he had gone she felt strangely comforted.

Katherine and Murry had often spoken of a friend of theirs in Paris, Francis Carco. Carco was a Bohemian poet boasting an extensive knowledge of the *demi-monde*. He seemed to have some strange fascination for Katherine.

It was some time after we had moved to St John's Wood that Katherine told me of how she was planning to leave Murry and go to Carco at Gray, where he was stationed in barracks in the military zone of France. Though she and Murry were not yet married, as her first husband had not divorced her, I had looked on them as inseparable and was worried about her. It seemed like one of her 'stunts'.

To convince me of the seriousness of her love affair with Carco, Katherine brought me one of his letters, but I felt she was trying to convince herself as well as me. Her plan to get permission to visit Carco was to pretend she was his wife, about to have a child, and she wanted to borrow a maternity dress of mine and wear a pillow under it. I do not think she made use of this idea; I pointed out that if it was discovered it might make things very difficult for her.

In her journal Katherine writes about the letter which she brought to me: 'I read and re-read the letter till it was all crumpled. Brigid half ate it in her mouth (Brigid was my baby). I loved her for that. She is the only person who has come anywhere near us just like that. I sat on the sofa and watched her little hands crunching the letter and felt she understood all about us and found us delicious.'

Katherine went to France about the middle of February 1915. She describes the difficulties of her journey in her journal and says how frightened she was: 'We arrived at Gray and one by one like women in to see a doctor, we slipped through a door into a hot room completely filled with two tables and two Colonels like Colonels in comic-opera, big shiny, grey-whiskered men with a touch of burnt-red in their cheeks.' After some questioning she finally got her passport stamped and was allowed to go on.

She describes how Carco was waiting for her at the station at Gray 'looking terribly pale'. He saluted and smiled and said, 'Turn to the right and follow me as though you were not following.' Then they took a cab and went to the house where he had taken a room for her. From then on it seemed to become a time of almost idyllic happiness for both of them, but very soon Katherine began to feel that there was something false about the whole affair. A few weeks later she came back to London, according to Murry, 'completely disillusioned'. None of us asked any questions; she was very silent and depressed. Later she wrote a short story, 'An Indiscreet Journey', which was obviously founded on the incident. During her absence Murry had spent most of his time with us, looking very white and miserable.

One morning about a year later I went round to Acacia Road to visit Katherine, and found her alone in the little top room where she used to write. There was a photograph of her brother 'Chummy' in uniform on her desk, who I knew had lately been in London on leave. She had always spoken happily about him and of their love for each other, for he seemed to be the one member of her family with whom she was absolutely in tune.

I took up the photograph to look at it and asked if she had heard from him since his leave. I noticed that she was looking at me in a queer, wild, hard way; then she said, 'Blown to bits!'

I was stunned. I asked when she had heard the news. She mentioned a date a few days previously. I remembered that she and Murry and Kot had come round to us that evening, and that Kot and Murry had been very silent but Katherine had seemed exceptionally talkative and gay. She had been wearing her embroidered shawl, which gave her a party air. Evidently she had told Kot and Murry not to mention her brother's death to us. It was as if the knowledge of his death was too terrible and unbelievable a fact to share with other people, until she had had time to face up to it alone and in some way accept it.

In the same year my brother Philip, who was in the R.A.M.C., was reported 'missing, believed killed', at Ypres. There were weeks of anxiety, hopes and fears, and heart-breaking letters from my mother. At last, very early one morning, a telegram arrived from my father: 'Philip a prisoner in Germany. Wounded in the knee.' That was happiness!

Gordon's youngest brother, Philip, was killed in 1916 at Beaumont-Hamel. Marjorie's young friends were nearly all killed in those first awful years of the war. These boys, barely out of school, went into action with very little training and not even the slight protection of a steel helmet. Marjorie was doing some sort of war-work in Ireland, and I felt she was going through a tragic time. I wished I could do something to help her.

One day a girl-friend of Gertler's from the Slade School who was known as 'Carrington' came to tell me about a plan to give a monster matinée in the Chelsea Palace Theatre in aid of Miss Lena Ashwell's Concerts for the Front. It seemed that everyone in the social, theatrical and intellectual world of London was to appear in it. Carrington was on one of the numerous committees among the duchesses and theatrical celebrities.

It was to be a sort of history of Chelsea, with little plays about Rossetti, Whistler and others, with songs and dances ending up with a grand finale in praise of Augustus John. Carrington's job was to collect a chorus of about forty people for the final scene. She was designing the dresses, which were to be made by Roger Fry's Omega Workshop. She had got a lot of distinguished names

83

for her chorus (but doubted whether any of them could sing), and asked me to join them. I was delighted, especially when she agreed to have Marjorie too. I told her how useful Marjorie would be as another voice and wired to Marjorie forthwith—Marjorie came.

The rehearsals started. They were held in any theatre where we could get a stage. We went from place to place; we missed nothing; we were in the wings, the stalls, the dressing-rooms, the green-rooms, very interested in all the celebrities we had come in contact with. Our song had six long verses with choruses, each chorus having different words. The words of the song were written by Harry Graham and the music by H. Fraser-Simson.

It began:

> Some people will squander their earnings away
> On paintings by Rankin and Steer,
> For Brangwyn or Condor huge sums they will pay,
> And they buy all the Prydes that appear.
> But if you'd be smart as patrons of art
> It's almost a *sine qua non*
> To prove your discretion by gaining possession
> Of works by the wonderful John.

At this point we came on, singing:

> John, John, how he's got on,
> He owes it, he knows it, to me.
> Brass ear-rings I wear and I don't do my hair
> And my feet are as bare as can be.
> When I walk down the street, the people I meet
> All stare at the things I've got on.
> When Battersea-Parking, you'll hear folks remarking,
> There goes an Augustus John.

Our producer, Harry Gratton, had at first tried to make us enter with little steps and kicks like a trained music-hall chorus, but the result was chaos. We kept kicking the people in front and in turn got kicked by those behind. Then we had the brilliant idea that we should slouch on and take poses about the stage like John's drawings.

84

The dress-rehearsal was a terrific occasion. It went on for hours. We wore little coloured coats and long skirts over bare feet, and had funny hats with high crowns or scarves tied round our heads. The chaos in the dressing-rooms was indescribable. An almost naked woman threw a black garment at me and shouted, 'For God's sake, sew me into this!' The garment was skin-tight and had a cat's head. While I sewed her up the side I found traces of oil-paint. I thought she must be a painter and when I had finished I hurried to get my programme to find out who she was. She was Nina Hamnett.

Ellen Terry was in the show as the 'Spirit of Chelsea'; she was accompanied by two of her grandchildren. She was very old and charming, and I think she had little idea what it was all about. The waits between the scenes were interminable. At last the time came for the great Augustus John finale. There was a heavy curtain all round the back of the stage, from behind which we were supposed to emerge after a soloist had sung the first verse. We stood behind this curtain waiting for our cue, but when the moment came no one knew where the opening in the curtain was and we wildly clawed round it, seized with panic. Finally we found it and the forty singers bundled on to the stage in a heap. Quickly we started singing and slouching and managed somehow to save the situation.

The show was such a financial success that they decided to repeat the performance in June of the same year. There were many new items bringing in more professional theatrical people, including some Russian dancers with Madame Seraphine Astavieva. I also remember Jack Buchanan, Violet Lorraine, Phyllis Monkman, Leslie Henson and Joseph Coyne. The second time we performed in the Lyric Theatre, and in one of the new items a young woman, not a professional, strolled up and down the stage singing in a very small voice, 'Love is the engine driver.' The wounded soldiers in their blue hospital uniforms in the upper circle sang:

> I want to go over the sea
> Where Allemands can't shoot at me.
> Oh my! I don't want to die,
> I want to go home.

The Commander-in-Chief, Field-Marshal Earl Haig of Bemersyde, wrote to thank the performers, saying the Concerts for the Front had been a source of endless pleasure and relaxation for many thousands of soldiers. I think the matinées in aid of them had been a source of some pleasure and relaxation to us too.

8

*Ill news from Ireland - Kot acquires an exceptional dog - I
survey ruins and review emotions - A London 'caravanserai' -
Lawrence loses a hat and makes an omelette - Letters from
wandering friends*

In Easter Week 1916 we heard of the Rising in Ireland. For several
days there was no connection with Dublin by telephone, telegram
or letter. We could only guess what was happening by questions
asked in the House of Commons, about 'Fighting in the streets',
'The city burning', 'Hundreds killed'. After some time letters began
to arrive from home and how eagerly we read them! Marjorie
had been to Fairy House Races with some friends on Easter Monday
and it had taken her four days to get back through Dublin to
Foxrock on foot. My parents meanwhile went nearly mad with
anxiety.

I had grown up with people like Sarah Purser who since the
time of Parnell had worked for Ireland, hoping to achieve Home
Rule and Independence by peaceful and constitutional means. John
Redmond had made what seemed a wise and generous gesture, and
I felt the matter could rest there till after the war. Now, suddenly,
there was killing and burning. Revolution which necessitated such
things could only be justified by terrible oppression and tyranny,
and there was none of that in Ireland.

It was about this time that Brigid, now known as 'Biddy', aged
two years, had an operation in a London nursing-home for appen-
dicitis. When she recovered, Alice and I and the two children
went to stay at a farmhouse which our friends the Hutchinsons
had rented in West Wittering. The two little Hutchinson children
came too, with their nurse. Barbara Hutchinson was about the
same age as Paddy, a funny freckle-faced little girl. Jeremy was
younger than Biddy, a fat little boy in a velvet suit. The farmhouse
was called 'Eleanors'. It was close to an inlet of the sea, and when

the tide went out it left behind it some rather beautiful mud-flats. The Hutchinsons had weekend parties at Eleanors with many young painters and writers of that time. Tonks, Duncan Grant and Vanessa Bell often made use of a large disused boathouse there as a studio.

In spite of what seemed almost, on the surface, a gay life in London, terrible things had been happening in all our lives owing to the war. I had not been in the country during the spring for several years. I distinctly remember the queer sense of comfort and healing I got from the fields and the sea, the smell of grass, primroses in the ditches, and the sudden lovely call of the cuckoo.

It was Whitsuntide, and Mary and 'Hutch', Montague Shearman, Gertler and Gordon came for the weekend. It must have been a warm spring, for I remember some of the party bathing on a very stony beach. I also remember the pleasure I got from the paintings that Duncan Grant had done on the panels of the doors of the farmhouse.

St John Hutchinson was a charmer. It was difficult to associate his laughter-loving air of good living with the rather grim fact that he was a very distinguished criminal lawyer. He was very interested in painting and had made a small collection of good contemporary work. Mary Hutchinson was also a charmer in her own more mysterious way. The Hutchinsons had a lovely house in Hammersmith, which had decorations in it by Duncan Grant, as well as some by Vanessa Bell and Roger Fry. They gave wonderful parties in which charades were a speciality. I remember one which included a scene in the Russian Court. 'Hutch' was a splendid Greek Church archbishop, Gilbert Cannan the Czar, Viola Tree the Czarina, Gertler the Czarevitch and Molly MacCarthy (Desmond MacCarthy's wife) was an English governess to the Czarevitch. Boris Anrep played Rasputin. The actors used anything they could to dress up in, as well as things supplied by Mary Hutchinson. I felt honoured when I recognized that a rather shabby fur stole of mine had been turned into a hat for the Czar.

Boris Anrep, years later, did the mosaics on the floors of the vestibules of the London National Gallery. Many distinguished people of that day are portrayed in them in delightful imaginative settings. Among them Mary Hutchinson appears as the Muse of Erotic Poetry.

After the death of Katherine's brother, she and Murry left Acacia Road. A Russian journalist, Michael Farbman, and his wife and daughter took the house, and Kot went to live with them. When, a few years later, the Farbman family went away Kot kept on the house and lived there till his death in 1955.

The Farbmans had a dog named Fox, who was the most intelligent, most sensitive and wisest dog in London. When the Zeppelins or German bombers crossed the South Coast and the outer barrage of London opened up, Fox would hear it long before anyone else, and would come and warn Kot. Many a raid they sat through together, giving courage to each other. When the 'All Clear' signals sounded Fox would rush round barking with joy.

While the Farbmans were still in Acacia Road, a Russian cousin, a refugee, came to stay with them. Kot disliked this man very much, and Mrs Farbman asked him jokingly, if either Fox or this cousin had to be 'liquidated', which would he choose. Kot at once said, 'Absolutely, emphatically, without a doubt, the cousin.' He believed Fox to be a far more valuable being in every way.

Some children who lived near Kot's house took a great fancy to Fox and he used to visit them. The children's mother went to Kot and asked him to lend them the dog for a month as they were leaving London after that time, so Kot agreed. At the end of the month Fox returned, but according to Kot he had become 'such a stupid fool' by living with 'ordinary' people that he had lost all his rare qualities. By degrees these qualities came back, and he was once again the most 'exceptional' dog in London. He lived for years, and Kot nursed him night and day in his last illness, when 'he died like a man'.

We were in Dublin in the summer of 1916, after the Easter Week Rising, and drove round looking at the ruins and hearing all the stories. I went to see Sarah Purser, who was bitter and resentful. She said, 'We have been put back a hundred years.' Later on, when the new régime began to function under W. T. Cosgrave's Government, she accepted it and worked as hard and as whole-heartedly for the new Ireland as she had done for the old.

While I was in the Stained Glass Works I had illustrated a child's book for Patrick Pearse, one of the leaders of the rising who had been court-martialled and shot. He was a rather bulky, pale, shy young man whose black clothes made him look as if he belonged to some religious order. As his book was in Irish and I did not understand the language, he used to come to my studio to translate the bits that he wanted me to make drawings for.

One day while he was there Sarah Purser came in and talked to him about the school for boys which he was starting. After he had gone she expressed some doubts about the wisdom of the political influence he would have on the boys under his care. Many years later P. S. O'Hegarty, who was himself a member of the Supreme Council of the Irish Republican Brotherhood, wrote the following: 'We adopted political assassination as a principle; we turned the whole thoughts and passions of a generation upon blood and revenge and death; we placed gunmen, mostly half-educated and totally inexperienced, as dictators with powers of life and death over large areas. We decided the moral law, and said there was no law but the law of force, and the moral law answered us. Every devilish thing we did against the British went its full circle, and then boomeranged and smote us tenfold; and the cumulating effect of the whole of it was a general moral weakening and a general degradation, a general cynicism and disbelief in either virtue or decency, in goodness or uprightness or honesty.'

Constance Markiewicz, another of the leaders, whose death-sentence was commuted to imprisonment, had been a member of the Arts Club with her very popular Polish painter husband Count Markiewicz. I remember her as a gay, adventurous young woman, whom no one at that time took very seriously either as a painter or a politician.

From the time when I started going to the School of Art I had found it almost too easy to become romantic and emotional about Irish politics. I had been very impressed by Yeats's *Cathleen ni Houlihan* and some early patriotic paintings by Jack Yeats. Irish patriotic songs and Irish patriotic poetry were very potent. It was difficult for a young, susceptible person not to be swept away in a flood of patriotism, but to be really involved in this movement it was necessary to have a great hate of England and everything English—I could never work myself up to that part of it.

While I was in the Stained Glass Works I had painted an allegorical picture of a seated, hooded figure of Cathleen ni Houlihan, with a child on her knee, presumably Young Ireland, stretching out his arm to the future, and behind her a ghostly crowd of martyrs, patriots, saints and scholars. Maud Gonne bought this picture and presented it to St Edna's College, the school for boys which Patrick Pearse had started. Some time later I met one of the boys from the school and he told me that this picture had inspired him 'to die for Ireland'! I was shocked at the thought that my rather banal and sentimental picture might, like Helen's face, launch ships and burn towers!

But to return to London. Our house in Norfolk Road seemed to be always full of soldiers and sailors. Alice had a sister, Minnie, who came to us as cook, and these two appeared to have an endless supply of brothers, all in the Army or Navy, who spent their leaves with us. The girls made up beds on the kitchen floor for the men, who seemed delighted to get away from anything which suggested barracks or 'quarters'.

Marjorie came to stay with us and got herself work with the Air Board. She brought friends and they brought their friends. It was hard to make the rations go round; but Alice was a great organizer, and everyone helped. I remember Goodyear, who had joined the Artists' Rifles, turning up with a hamper of unrationed luxuries from Fortnum and Mason's, which was very welcome. Kot said, 'Your house is not a home, it is a caravanserai.'

When I think of people in the past, I see them in my mind, not static, not as 'stills', but as moving pictures. Kot is putting slices of lemon into the tea-cups, he is holding the slice between his thumb and the tip of a teaspoon. Katherine is talking and making a slight gesture with one hand, holding her fingers upwards in the shape of a cup and moving her hand up and down. Gertler is tossing his head backwards in laughter. Lawrence is thumping the back of a chair and denouncing everyone, including himself— though he never made that part of it very evident.

I seldom saw Lawrence apart from Frieda, whose over-vital and noisy presence usually reduced him to a gentle, bearded shadow. He had a frail appearance, with a shock of thick, almost rough, 'sandy' hair, but his eyes seemed to have a life of their own, like two lonely, intense, suspicious animals looking out from the caves of his eye-sockets. He and Frieda were so often involved in some terrible quarrel that I rather dreaded being left alone with them. Also they both wanted to pry into one's private life and ask personal questions.

I once left the sitting-room where Lawrence was preaching furiously and found in the hall my little boy Paddy, with a very guilty look on his face. I asked him what mischief he had been up to and he said, 'I hided his hat.' He showed me where he had put Lawrence's rather odd straw hat, under some coats in a cupboard. I found it almost a pleasure to be in a conspiracy against Lawrence.

There was another pleasant moment at No. 5, Acacia Road, when Lawrence made an omelette and it rose up so high in the frying-pan in a mountain of foam that he called us all down to the kitchen to see it. It was then carried in triumph to the next room to be eaten. Just as all seemed happy, something suddenly annoyed Lawrence and he said furiously, 'Everyone must change wives. Kot can have Beatrice and Gertler can have Frieda.' In a minute Frieda was attacking Lawrence and everything was spoilt.

Lawrence took a great pride in the fact that Frieda was a daughter of Baron von Richthofen, of the ancient house of Richthofen. He described the Richthofens in a letter in 1912 as 'an astonishing family, three girls—the father a fierce old aristocrat—mother utterly non-moral, very kind'. Katherine once said that Lawrence was made up of three people: the black devil whom she hated, the preacher whom she did not believe in, and the artist whom she loved and valued. Though it took these three different sides of him to make the whole man, it was difficult ever to get in touch with the artist.

Lawrence and Frieda, Katherine and Murry were always going away and coming back again. At one time all four of them went to live at Zennor in Cornwall. The Lawrences had gone there first. They had taken a cottage and then found another one near by in which they persuaded the Murrys to come and live. Katherine wrote to me from there:

My dear Bici,

I want to ask you for that prescription for poor Murry's remaining hair. For though he is about to be taken he must rub something into his roots while he is on sentry go—send it when you find it.

If I had a box I'd send you flowers but I've nothing but a Vinolia soap box and the violets would arrive in a lather. As soon as I have a box you shall have some. This country is very lovely just now with every kind of little growing thing—and the gorse amongst the grey rocks is, as Mrs Percy W. (Hutchinson) would agree, very satisfactory. There are a great many adders here too. How does one cure oneself of their bite? You either bathe the afflicted part with a saucer of milk *or* you give the milk to the adder.

There is a creek close by our house that rushes down a narrow valley and then falls down a steep cliff into the sea—the banks are covered with primroses, violets and bluebells. I paddle in it and feel like a faint far-off reflection of the George Meredith Penny-Whistle Overture, but awfully faint.

Murry spends all his time hunting for his horn-rimmed spectacles, for whenever he leaps over a stile or upon a mossy stone they fly from him, incredible distances, and undergo a strange and secret change into caterpillars, dragon-flies and bracken uncurling.

Today I can't see a yard—thick mist and rain and a tearing wind with it. Everything is faintly damp, the floor of the tower is studded with Cornish pitchers catching the drops. Except for my little maid (whose *ankles* I can hear clumping about the kitchen) I'm alone—for Murry and Lawrence have plunged off to St Ives with rucksacks on their backs and Frieda is in her cottage looking at the children's photographs, I suppose. It is very quiet in the house except for the wind and rain and the fire that roars very hoarse and fierce.

I feel as though I and the Cornish Pasty had drifted out to

93

sea—and would never be seen again. but I love such days—rare lovely days. I love above all things, my dear, to be alone. Then I lie down and smoke and look at the fire and begin to think out an EXTRAORDINARILY good story about Marseilles. I've re-read my novel today and now I can't believe I wrote it. I hope that Gordon reads it one of these days.

I want to talk about the L's. But if I do don't tell Kot or Gertler for then it will get back to Lawrence and I will be literally murdered. He has changed very much. He's quite 'lost'. He has become very fond of sewing, especially hemming, and of making little copies of pictures. When he is doing these things he is quiet and gentle and kind, but once you start talking I cannot describe the frenzy that comes over him. He simply *raves*, roars and beats the table, abuses everybody. It is impossible to be anything to him but a kind of playful acquaintance. Frieda is more or less used to this. She has a passion for washing clothes —and looking very much at home indeed. She says this place suits her. I am sure it does. They are both too tough for me to enjoy playing with. I hate games where people lose their tempers in this way—it's so witless. In fact they are not my kind at all. I cannot discuss blood affinity to beasts for instance, if I have to keep ducking to avoid the flat-irons and the saucepans. And I *shall never* see sex in trees, sex in running brooks, sex in stones and sex in everything. The number of things that are really phallic, from fountain pens onwards! But I shall have my revenge one of these days—I suggested to Lawrence that he should call his cottage 'The Phallus' and Frieda thought it a very good idea. It's lunchtime already and here is the pastry looming through the mist with a glimmering egg on a tray. Have you read so far? Give my dear love to Gordon and keep it yourself,

Katherine.

Some time later Frieda also wrote from Cornwall, shortly after *Women in Love* had been published. In it there was a very cruel portrait of Lady Ottoline as a woman called Hermione Roddice, and Ottoline had been offended and hurt by it. Frieda's letter is to Gordon, and says:

Dear Campbell,

How you enjoy writing those letters of yours. Lawrence looks so tickled and exasperated with them. You must read the novel, it will be sardonic enough for you even—the 'Ott' read it—was furious, wrote as a vulgar cook who writes to her young man. She asked for an opal pin back she had given him!! Lawrence wrote and said, 'No, you have given it me, I keep it, be more careful another time to whom you give your friendship so freely!' But I rise like the Phoenix, like seven Phoenixes, I know her cheap spirituality, with her adoration of young geniuses, she is only a flapper in herself! Things between me and the children are adjusting themselves. There is a connection anyhow. L and I are really happy, we have got somewhere onto a bed-rock—I am happy and no longer the damned miserable, whining bloody female that bored everybody about her brats—I used to think you beastly unsympathetic, you said such commonsense hard things. I think one's affection for Katherine M. is a kind of vice, we have not heard from her since October, in fact it is over, but if she comes this minute I would have to be nice with her. She has the terrible gift of nearness, she can come so close, but it's really no good in the long run! I wish you would come and see us! It would do you good to have the wind blow through you like it does here! Please give Beatrice my affection, how is she, and how does she put up with you? I *am* a daisy in *Mendel*, I must say! I am happy! I am going to get out—*blast* all old bosh!

> Yours affectionately,
> Frieda.

In this letter Frieda alludes to a novel called *Mendel* by Gilbert Cannan. Mendel was Gertler, the book was about Gertler and his friends, including a long account of his unhappy love-affair with Carrington; everyone was in it, quite recognizable but under a different name. Lawrence wrote of it, saying, 'Gertler has told every detail of his life to Gilbert. Gilbert has a lawyer's mind and has put it all down. It is a bad book, statement without creation—really journalism.'

I had another letter from Katherine in Cornwall, and I am still moved by the feeling of friendliness and affection which it contains:

Ma très Chére,

I have been waiting for the time and the place to answer you in, and they both seem here. So thank you for the prescription (which you shall have back) and for your letter and the papers. We have just been talking about you and Gordon—I hope your ears kept up a pleasant burning for we are awfully fond of you always, Gordon is quite sincerely and for ever Murry's only love, but Gordon knows that.

It is Sunday evening. Sometimes I feel I'd like to write a whole book of short stories and call each one 'Sunday'. Does Sunday mean to you something vivid and strange and remembered with longing—the description sounds rather like the habits contracted by Jean Jacques Rousseau when his blood was inflamed by his youth—or like Gordon lying on his bed reading the police court news—but I don't mean that. Sunday is what these talking people call a rare state of consciousness—and what I would call —the feeling that sweeps me away when I *hear* an *unseen* piano. Yes, that's just it, and now I come to think of it, isn't it extraordinary how many pianos come into being only on Sunday. Lord! someone, heaven knows who, starts playing something like Mendelssohn's Melodia in F—or miles away some other one plays a funny little Gavotte by Beethoven that you simply can't bear. I feel about an unknown piano, my dear, what certain men feel about unknown women—no question of love—but simply 'an uncontrollable desire to stalk them'—not that there is even the ghost of a pianner here. Nothing but the clock and the fire and sometimes a gust of wind breaking over the house. This house is very like a house left high and dry. It has the same 'hollow' feeling—the same big beams and narrow doors and passages that only a fish could swim through without touching and the little round windows at the back are just like port-holes—which reminds me—there has been a calf lying under the dining-room window all day. Has anyone taken it in? It has

8 SOUTH BOLTON GARDENS. S.W.
KENSINGTON 2811.

*what are the wild waves saying, sister the whole day long.?
anyway Brid jit They don't seem to be saying anything
to you about your one time little friend above – But
even so my darling I wish you and yours all happiness,
and its honest I would like to see your ugly mug again
with much love Orpit*

A self-portrait by William
Orpen in a letter to the author,
about 1923
The letter reads: *What are the
wild waves saying, sister the
whole day long? Anyway
Bridgit they don't seem to be
saying anything to you about
your one time little friend
above—But even so my
darling I wish you and yours
all happiness, and its honest
I would like to see your ugly
mug again. With much love
Digit*

William Orpen, about 1914

A passport photograph of
Koteliansky as a young man

S. S. Koteliansky at 5 Acacia Road, 1935

S. S. Koteliansky with Jonathan Stoye, H. G. Wells's grandson, 5 Acacia Road, 1951

been another misty day. Highland Cattle crossing the stream by Landseer and the little calf has lain shivering and wondering what to do with its far too big head all day long. What time its mother has guzzled and chewed away and looked into the distance and wondered if she were too fat to wear a tussore coat like any Christian woman. If the calf were only something smaller I could send my soul out wrapped in a non-existent shawl and carrying a non-existent basket lined with non-existent flannel and bring it in to the dead-out kitchen fire to get warm. I must stop this letter, write to me again very soon, Bici. Love,

Katherine.

The strain of living next door to the Lawrences proved too exhausting for the Murrys. Katherine soon went back to London and stayed in different places, while Murry looked for another cottage on the south side of Cornwall. He found one which he liked very much, and Katherine wrote to me:

Dearest Bici,

I am going to Cornwall on Monday to Sunnyside Cottage, Mylor, near Penryn. I will write to you from there, do write to me too darling, and tell me the news. I arrived at Paddington to find the station crowded with Sinn Feiners who had just arrived from Wormwood Scrubs and were being taken, on the points of innumerable bayonets to some other prison. Heavens! what a sight it was—but they all looked very happy and they all wore bunches of green ribbon and green badges—I very nearly joined them, and I rather wish I had. In great haste, darling, thank you again for my bed.

Always,
Mansfield.

I often wish I could talk to Katherine now. We would have such a lot to say to each other about everything and everybody. Though I was older than she was, in those days she was far ahead of me in what she called 'experience'.

Gordon had a way of talking about people which delighted Katherine and Murry. It was a mixture of fantasy and mockery but done without malice, they called it 'Campbelling'. 'To Campbell' became almost an art; they all tried it, but its finer points were so completely an Irish form of humour that they finally left it to Gordon to indulge in alone.

Lawrence wrote to him soon after they first met: 'How did you get on with Koteliansky? He says of you "He is quite simple, really a simple man. When he is cynical, it is nothing. He knows—he knows." '

On January 22, 1917, Lawrence wrote to Gordon from Cornwall:

I want to go clean away, for ever. I feel it is finished in me, with this side of the globe . . . I hope in the long run to find a place where one can live simply, apart from this civilisation, on the Pacific, and have a few other people who are also at peace and happy and live, and understand, and be *free* . . . Don't mind my previous censures. You are a man who *can* understand—but you don't want to sacrifice the world. I hope you will one day . . . Have you heard of Murry lately? You seem to be the only man left in England, to whom I can say even so much as in this letter . . .

Later Lawrence wrote, in an undated letter, with no address:

You shouldn't think we don't like you, and things like that. We detest you sometimes, as you detest us. But I feel as if I need you to understand the things I can't understand myself. There are very few people whom I need *extremely*—because very few people could help. But Murry—& you—and perhaps E. M. Forster. As for Philip Morrell & Lady O—they are good, genuine souls—but not fighters or leaders.

You see for this thing which I stutter at so damnably I want us to form a league—you and Murry and me and perhaps Forster—& our women—& anyone who will be added on to us —so long as we are centred around a core of reality, and carried on one impulse.

This letter was probably written about 1915 when Lawrence began to formulate his ideas about an Isle of the Blest which he had named Rananim (a name which he got out of one of Kot's Hebrew songs). He had written out a long draft for the constitution of this island and given it to Gordon to study, hoping to get him interested and involved, believing him to have the organizing capacity and the capital to work the scheme. Gordon put the papers away and they were forgotten till after Lawrence's death when Gordon met Aldous Huxley in London and they spoke of Lawrence, and Gordon remembered the plans for the island which his practical mind had not taken seriously. Huxley was very interested and said these papers were of great importance and interest. When Gordon returned home he looked for them in the place where he thought he had put them, but they were not there. We searched the house and we almost tore it to bits in an effort to find the document, which consisted of several sheets of paper covered with Lawrence's own beautifully careful writing. They were never found and their disappearance remains a mystery.

9

Entertaining in North-west London - Kot pronounces and
is pronounced upon - Two Russians in a rage - I witness
an orgy of destruction - 'Black moods' and revolutions - Cheers
echo to a crimson sky - Bombers over the horse-chestnut -
We brave the Irish Sea - A visit by masked men - Privation
in Gloucestershire and plenty in Surrey

After Katherine, Murry, Lawrence and Frieda had left London, Kot
and Gertler remained faithful to our Sunday evenings. Our Irish
cook used to allude to them as 'them Roosshians'. The kitchen in
Norfolk Road was under the room where we sat and talked. Sometimes there would be a great noise going on down below, the
range being cleaned out, much banging and clattering, and loud
conversation between the cook and the children's nurse. I remember Gertler saying, 'I wish those Irish servants would eat their
potato and go to bed.'

At this time Gertler was living at No. 19, Worsley Road, Hampstead, and had a studio in Rudall Crescent. He remained there
for about fifteen years. His landlady had been a housekeeper in
some stately home, who on retirement had taken a small house
with room for one lodger. Never was a lodger more assiduously
cared for or better looked after. I remember going to dinner with
him there when other members of the party were Lady Ottoline,
Kot, W. J. Turner and his wife Delphine. The dinner was so perfectly cooked and served that even Ottoline, who was more
accustomed to gracious living than the rest of us, congratulated
him.

Kot still issued pronouncements on people and things in general
which I enjoyed very much; they were so emphatic and final.
There were no half-measures; he would say of someone, 'He is a
liar and a swindler', or 'The Irish are fleas and lice', or 'Ninety-
five per cent of the human race are manure.' I once said to W. J.
Turner how wonderful it was to have someone like Kot to whom

you could bring every problem, every question, and get a definite explanation or plain answer, and added that I believed that whatever Kot said was right. Turner looked astonished and said, 'But I don't think Kot is ever right about anything.'

One had a sense, with Kot, of being up against something which could not tolerate even the shadow of a lie. One night at the St John Hutchinson's in Hammersmith there was talk about how impossible it was for anyone to be absolutely truthful, and how no one could be quite incapable of telling a lie. Gertler and I looked at each other, both thinking of Kot, then Gertler plunged into the discussion and we both wildly affirmed that in Kot's presence a lie could not exist, that his moral integrity made other people seem like ghosts.

Gertler told of incidents between himself and Kot to prove this. He said Kot was quite unconscious of his truth-making effect on other people, but it was profound. He went on to say that at times he bitterly resented this power in Kot. 'I feel, in self-defence, I have to fight against him. I want to be a lie, and to tell lies. I will be a lie if I like.' Gertler then rather destroyed everything by saying, 'If Kot wants to deceive himself no one can practise deception more superbly than Kot, but that would take seven hours to explain.' As it was then past midnight, we left. Outside in the foggy night, waiting for a taxi, we spoke almost in a whisper, saying, 'How awful if Kot knew that we had been discussing him with other people!'

Gilbert Cannan had left Mary and was living with a girl known as 'Plucky'. He had used this word to describe her courage in living a rather unconventional life. I think it was Gertler's sense of the ridiculous which made it a nickname for her. 'Plucky' had some very rich Jewish friends and she invited us all to go to a party in their luxurious flat. I must mention here that Kot had some peculiar complex which sometimes made him think it rather fine to be rude to people whom he considered rich, and that if they accepted his rudeness he had gained a victory over them. We went to the party.

Our hostess introduced Kot to another Russian, and we left them talking Russian together in a small room with a blue ceiling and large silver stars on it. There was dancing in a larger room. During the evening Gertler and I went to see how Kot was getting on, to find him and the other Russian in a terrible rage with each other. When Kot saw us he jumped up and, pushing his way through all the dancers, made for the hall-door, saying in a loud voice, 'Why do we waste ourselves on these rubbishy people?' We all followed him, delighted to get away, though it was a very grand party. Kot's hate was a terrible thing, but to a chosen few he used to give his very rare brand of friendship.

A friend of Gertler's, Montague Shearman, picture-collector and connoisseur, had a large room in the Adelphi, comfortably furnished, with books, pianola, pictures, gramophone and a cocktail cabinet. He gave a key of this room to several of his intimate friends, including Gertler, so that they could use it when they liked.

While the Russian Ballet was still having its season in London, Kot and Gertler, Gordon and I dined somewhere and afterwards Gertler suggested going to Shearman's room, which we did. On opening the door, we were surprised to find the whole place arranged for a party. There were flowers everywhere and every sort of delicacy—sandwiches and cakes, bottles of wine, decanters and liqueurs, even a large bottle of eau-de-Cologne. We guessed that Shearman was at the ballet with a party, and would be bringing them back, probably Lopokova, Diaghilev and half the company, after the show.

For some extraordinary reason which has never been explained, Kot and Gertler seemed to go raving mad. It was really Kot who started it. They dashed at the bottles and the liqueurs, drinking everything and eating all the sandwiches, holding them madly in both hands. They threw the flowers and cushions all over the place and Kot took a painted wooden tray made by Roger Fry at the Omega Workshop and smashed it down with both hands over Gertler's head. I can still see Gertler's startled, delighted expression. The wooden rim of the tray hung round his shoulders like a collar, as he leaped about over the furniture shaking the eau-de-Cologne everywhere. Kot was fiercely serious, Gertler was hysterical with laughter and exaltation at taking a part in something so outrageous. Gordon kept well away at the far end of the room, also laughing. I was horrified and implored Gordon to stop them wrecking the place. Kot rushed at the pianola, which had a roll ready for playing, and played it absolutely *fortissimo* and terribly fast.

Suddenly there was a furious knocking at the door. We opened it, and there was a very angry man from another room in a fearful rage over the appalling noise, threatening to call the police. After that we left, Gertler suggesting that we should go to the place where Gilbert Cannan and 'Plucky' had a studio. We went there and found a party going on, with dancing. Kot would not come into the studio. He sat in a sort of courtyard and moaned. His glasses had been broken during the 'incident' and whenever we went out to see how he was, he would say in despair, 'The glasses are broke, hey?'

Gertler was quite sober. Kot had done all the drinking. We had great difficulty in getting him home, for he clung to the railings and lamp-posts, moaning, 'The glasses are broke, hey?' We got him, at last, to No. 5, Acacia Road, and put him through his halldoor, where he collapsed. As we walked away in silence, Gertler said, 'That Kot should be drunk! It is as if the bottom had fallen out of everything, as if everything had come to an end.'

We did not see Kot again for some time. Gertler said, 'He is having a black mood.' Shearman merely wrote a polite note to Gertler asking him to return the key. After Gertler's death, Shearman went to Kot to make some arrangements for having an exhibition of Gertler's paintings. Kot admired him very much for never mentioning the 'incident' and not bearing any ill-will about the destruction of the Russian Ballet party.

I think none of us knew or understood Kot's feelings about Russia at that time. In 1917 there had been the 'bloodless revolution'. The Czar had abdicated, and the Provisional Government had taken over, with Kerensky at its head. When Kot first got this news, he went to an old Russian friend of his, the widow of a leader of the Russian Revolutionary Party, who wrote under the name of 'Stepniak'. Kot and old Madame Stepniak were so happy for Russia; it was as if all their dreams had come true. They walked the streets of London all night till the dawn. This triumphant mood did not last long. There came the second revolution, when the Bolshevik Party took over and Kerensky had to fly for his life. Kot's mother and brothers and sisters and other members of his family were still in the Ukraine. There was murder, fighting and starvation. Kot did not speak of it, but this must have been a terrible time for him. We carried on with our own lives and our own war without paying much attention to his.

One Sunday night in 1916, Kot, Gertler and Carrington were with us. The talk must have been very absorbing, for we had no idea that a Zeppelin raid was going on. At the end of the evening Gordon went to the hall-door to see Kot and Gertler out. I had gone to make up a bed for Carrington in the study as it was too late for her to go home. Gordon came back saying that there were a lot of searchlights about, which was queer as we had not heard any guns. I went up to my room and was taking off my ear-rings when suddenly the whole outside world seemed to burst into a roar of fierce, terrible, savage cheering.

Pulling the curtains apart, I saw the whole sky was crimson and all the houses and trees lit up. I went down the stairs like an avalanche, gasping, 'Zeppelin coming down—burning.' Carrington shot out of her room, and we both clawed at the hall-door and dashed out into Norfolk Road. There it was, creeping and dripping down the sky, head first, mighty and majestic, a great flaming torch, and away up above it the little light of the plane, signalling to the guns. There was an Artillery barracks at the end of our road. The great roars of cheering, rising and falling in crescendo and diminuendo, came from there, but it sounded as if all London was cheering.

Carrington burst into terrible sobbing and rushed back to her room. I felt almost unconscious with excitement, and was on a plane of living where human suffering no longer existed. It looked as if the remains of the Zeppelin had come down on Hampstead Heath, though in reality it was much farther off, in rural Essex. I wanted to get a taxi and go to where it had fallen, and went to Carrington to get her to come with me, but she was crying so bitterly she could not speak, so I left her. The night was full of the honking of motor-horns. Everyone seemed to have gone to the spot. Next morning there were three miles of traffic-jam leading to the place.

There were many Zeppelin raids. After them came the bombing planes. The first time was in the morning of 17 July 1917. Marjorie and I were in the garden with the children, when we heard a great roaring in the sky. We ran out into the road to get a better view and were greeted by a most wonderful sight. In the distance, apparently coming up Norfolk Road, at a great height, were twenty-five German bombers, all glittering in the sunshine and flying in close formation. I ran back to collect the two children and the maids and get them into the basement. Marjorie followed a few seconds later, saying cheerfully, 'They are over the horse-chestnut tree at the gate now!' I remember no anti-aircraft guns, and the planes at that time were not dropping bombs; they just seemed to be making a tour of London.

I recently found an old photograph taken in the back garden of our house that afternoon. In it there is Humbert Wolfe, Amber Blanco White, Malcolm (who has been wounded and was on leave from France), Marjorie, the two children and myself. We all look so happy, as if such things as war and bombs simply did not exist.

Every summer Alice and I and the two children went back to Ireland for holidays. Sometimes Marjorie or Gordon came too. When I look back on this it seems like madness, for there were German submarines in the Irish Sea. Alice and I, with the two children sitting on our knees, all wearing cork life-belts, stayed on deck and scanned the sea for periscopes. The crossing took a long time as the boat did not take a straight course, but zig-zagged for greater safety.

In Ireland, the 'Troubles' were still going on. Houses of families whose sons were known to be in the British Army were being raided for arms and military equipment. Malcolm and Ronald were home on leave and, one night, while we were staying in my father's house, we heard a knock on the hall-door. In a second the room was full of masked men with revolvers, saying, 'Hold up your hands' and 'Don't move or you will be shot'. We had been playing some card game; we went on playing. My mother just looked up from her knitting and continued to knit, my father pretended to go on reading his newspaper.

I heard a commotion in the hall and Alice loudly exclaiming, 'I will *not* hold up my hands, and I *will* go to the children!' I went to her and together we reached the children's room. A masked man stood guard at the door. Biddy was fast asleep, but Paddy was awake and frightened. In those days we had only candlelight in our bedrooms, and the man looked very terrifying, with a black handkerchief round his face, a hat pulled well down and a revolver. I said, 'You are frightening the child. Take that thing off your face, come into the light and show Paddy your gun.' The young man did as I asked and said gently, 'Sure we wouldn't hurt you, Paddy.' They made a great collection of things on the landing—tin hats, Sam Brownes, water-bottles, field-glasses.

The Captain was the only one who was behaving like a real gunman, shouting, 'Silence' and 'Stand back' if anyone spoke or moved. What they were really looking for must have been a heavy service revolver belonging to the New Zealander whom Marjorie was going to marry. The maid may have told them that it was in the house. The only light they carried was a smoky oil bicycle-lamp, and between the excitement of bundling up all their loot and the lack of illumination they went off leaving the big revolver on Marjorie's bed. They said 'Good night' and we said 'Good night', and they warned us not to leave the house for two hours or we would be shot. The whole business had an air of almost comic unreality about it.

We had other raids, in broad daylight, when they came for medical books and first-aid equipment belonging to Philip's R.A.M.C. kit. We always parted the best of friends, and they never took anything that was not connected with their job of making Ireland 'free'.

We were staying near Dublin with my father-in-law when the *Leinster* was sunk. We might well have been on her, but the weather had been bad and we put off our departure till it improved to avoid the long rough crossing. Back in London, we found the air-raids were getting heavier and more frequent. I remember us all sitting in the kitchen singing loudly, 'Take me back to dear old Blighty' to hide the noise of the guns and falling bombs from the children.

To get away from air-raids we were lent a little house in Chipping Campden, in Gloucestershire. It was in the very middle of the main street, and was owned by Mrs Amber Blanco White (who had been the original of Ann Veronica in H. G. Wells's book), then working in Gordon's office in the Ministry of Munitions. Chipping Campden was beautiful. Our house dated from the fourteenth century, and the doors were so low that Alice and I had bruised and battered heads from passing through them. I had to put a notice over each door, reading, 'Mind your head.' The only other drawback was that we could not get anything to eat. The village shops would not sell us food as they had only enough for their usual customers. Alice used to go out shopping and come back with nothing but apples. My mother sent us tea, butter, rashers and other things from Ireland and they were all stopped in the post.

We finally went back to London and another of Gordon's secretaries lent us a house in Limpsfield in Surrey. This was a wonderful place. There was a kindly cook-housekeeper and plenty of food. I remember at our first meal Alice ate three platefuls of corned beef and cabbage. There was snow on the ground that day, the sun shone and the sky was blue. We found toboggans in the house and Alice and the children had a grand time. Away in the distance was the dull thud of the guns in France.

IO

*I become a war-worker - My sole excursion into oratory - A
Zeebrugge hero on leave - Jubilation and consternation -
Armistice week encounters - Katherine Mansfield prepares
a Last Supper - From influenza to Ireland - I reason
with incendiaries - The fire brigade drives us into exile
Gun-fire and philosophy*

For the last six months of the war we had a furnished cottage at
Oxted, near Limpsfield in Surrey. I worked in a War Depot,
making swabs and pneumonia jackets and rolling bandages. We
wore large white aprons and had white things on our heads, like
nurses, and we sat working at a long table. Everyone knew everyone else and everyone talked a lot. I knew no one and remained
silent.

I was interested in how all my fellow workers condemned a
woman who had given food to German prisoners working on her
land. She had given them cocoa and sandwiches, and said half of
them were 'mere children'. They arrived very early in charge of a
sergeant and got nothing to eat all day. The sergeant was glad to
see them fed, but the practice was stopped as it was against the
law.

As Oxted was part of the outer barrage of London, we often
had very noisy nights when German planes came over, but no
bombs were dropped; they were saving them for London, where
Marjorie and Gordon were.

At that time things were going badly for the Allies in France.
There had been much talk in the House of Commons about con-
scription for Ireland, which was being opposed by the Irish Members. The talk in the Depot got very bitter: 'The cowards, they
let us fight for them.' They harked back to 1916: 'The stab in
the back.' I stood it for a while in silence, then I felt my heart
beginning to beat like mad and a roaring in my ears. I felt my
face turning crimson.

I stood up and made the only speech I ever made in my life. I said, 'The Irish people are only doing what you English would do if you had been conquered by Germany.' I went on to say that in the cottage where I lived, I and my husband and our two maids represented four Irish families. Out of these four families there were ten brothers in the services and none of them was a conscript. I described the casualties among them, the killed, the wounded and the decorated. The ladies sat spellbound.

There was absolute silence as I got up and left the room. When I went to take off my apron and head-dress in the dressing-room I saw my face in the glass and I did not recognize myself. About a week later one of the ladies came to our cottage and said they were all so sorry, they 'didn't know I was Irish'. She implored me to go back, as I had been their best worker.

Alice had a young brother in the British Navy who had volunteered for the Zeebrugge affair, the plan to counter the submarine menace by sinking ships to block the canal entrances at Zeebrugge and Ostend. Of course, the volunteers had no idea of what they were in for; they were only told that it was 'very important, very dangerous and very secret'. For weeks beforehand they were trained and cared for 'as if they were going to run in the Derby'.

When the great night came, 22 April, 1918, he found himself working as a stoker on one of the blockships. He just went on stoking from the moment they left Dover, not knowing what was happening. After some time there were a lot of explosions and he found himself in the sea; he kept on swimming till he was picked up by a motor-launch. Then he fell asleep from exhaustion and woke up to discover himself back in Dover. It was all over. He had three weeks' leave, which he spent in our cottage sitting by the kitchen fire playing a concertina. I often urged Alice to take him up to London, to a theatre or to a cinema, but she said he was perfectly happy where he was.

While we were in Oxted I used to go up to London to see Kot and Gertler and sometimes they came down to us and stayed the night. I remember Kot trying to play with the children in the garden. He became a bear and leaped about on all fours, growling and snarling. The children were terrified and ran to me for safety, whereupon he seemed very hurt and said sadly, 'Russian children would have liked it.'

We were back in London again for the Armistice. At 11 o'clock on the morning of 11 November 1918 the maroons went off for the 'cease fire'. It was almost unbelievable! The war was over. Paddy came running in from the garden saying, 'Lottie Venne is hanging out her Union Jack.' Lottie Venne had been a famous music-hall star and now lived opposite us.

Gordon and Marjorie had gone to their offices, so we shut up the house, the two maids went off on their own, and I and the two children took a taxi to go to Gordon's office in Whitehall Gardens to join in the rejoicing. The children had Union Jacks, the taxi hood was open and they waved and cheered all the way. As we got nearer to Piccadilly Circus it was obvious that all London was rapidly going mad. Work had completely stopped and every form of transport was covered with yelling, cheering people; they were even heaped on the tops of taxis.

I felt I had better get the children home as soon as possible, so we cut short our visit to Whitehall and went to look for a bus or cab to get us back to St John's Wood. It was completely hopeless. I remember standing on an island at the foot of the Haymarket with the two frightened children, watching the roaring sea of traffic sweeping round us. There was nothing for it but to walk home and I set off slowly, first carrying one child then the other.

It began to rain slightly, which was refreshing, and after what seemed like hours of struggling we got to Baker Street Station. The buses were running normally at this point, but there were hundreds of people like us, all trying to get home. It was only by carrying a child in each arm and crying out that we had walked from White-hall, that room was eventually made for us in a bus and helping hands got us aboard.

In other people's memoirs of those days I have read varying accounts of Armistice night in Shearman's room, with lists of completely different people. The explanation of this is that 'Armistice night' went on for a week and there were different people in the room every night. The night we were there Henry Mond, in his singlet, played the pianola, people pouring champagne over him to keep him cool. Augustus John appeared, amid cheers, in his British officer's uniform, accompanied by some land-girls in leggings and breeches who brought a fresh feeling of the country into the overheated room. There was dancing and Gertler did a sort of Russian Ballet turn with Marjorie, who had found the room too hot, like Henry Mond, and had taken off her dress.

Later that week Marjorie and I went out alone at night to join the crowds. In Piccadilly Circus I saw her swept off into a dance with some sailors; everyone seemed to be kissing her. A man in a bowler hat approached me with outspread arms, but I must have given him a terrible look for he sheered away calling out, 'You 'ave got a koind fice, you 'ave'! Evidently I had no talent for public rejoicing.

At the time of the Armistice, Katherine and Murry were living in a house in Hampstead which they called 'The Elephant' because it was so big and grey. She had been very ill but as usual had been travelling about all over the place. They gave a small party—Kot, Gertler, Gordon and me. We had not seen her for some time and she looked terribly thin and frail. It was some comfort to know that Ida Baker was there looking after her.

It must have been Christmas time, as Katherine had prepared a tiny Christmas tree with little bags of sweets for each of us which she cut off and solemnly handed round. It was a sort of Last Supper. Kot, I felt, disliked it very much, for it seemed like one of Katherine's 'stunts', which in spite of his profound admiration and affection for her he strongly disapproved of. Things became more cheerful later on and we had charades, at which Gertler was very good. Kot would only act a dead man when it came to his turn.

Katherine and Murry went away from London soon after this. She had started a new treatment in Paris with a Russian, Dr Manoukhin. Her last visit to London was in 1922, by which time we had gone back to live in Ireland, and Kot wrote to me saying how happy he was about her and that he really believed she would be cured. She looked so well and had put on weight and was her old gay self again. They were having long talks over Russian tea at his kitchen table. He wrote: 'Katherine is almost perfect.' She went back to Paris and somehow lost faith in Dr Manoukhin's treatment, joined Gurdjieff's spiritual brotherhood in Fontaine-bleau, and died there in 1923.

Katherine had made herself a master of the short story. She published very few books during her lifetime, but after her death Murry added to her already established reputation by publishing her *Journal* and *Letters*, as well as other books of her poems and stories.

After the war we decided to go back to live in Dublin. Gordon had started a brilliant career at the Parliamentary Bar but he did not want to continue it, and I had always longed to live per-manently in Ireland. Before we left the great influenza epidemic struck London. Gordon somehow escaped it and went to his job every day, but Marjorie was seriously ill with the septic pneumonia variety of infection and the two children and the maids had the ordinary kind; I nursed them.

It was a terrible time—even our doctor died. Fortunately we were able to get another doctor, who was so attractive that Alice said it was all she could do not to kiss the back of his neck when he was bending over the children in their little beds. Eventually every-one recovered from the 'flu and we all packed up to go back to Dublin where Gordon had a post in the Ministry of Industry and Commerce of the Cosgrave Government. We had let the London house furnished for some months, and our furniture was to follow us later. Kot and Gertler came to Euston to say good-bye. They looked so desolate standing there on the platform that I felt I was leaving my two children behind and promised to go back and see them every year and write to them once a week for ever.

After wartime London it seemed as if Ireland would be a land of peace and plenty. We stayed in my father-in-law's house for a while and then moved about from one furnished house to another till we found a house of our own.

My father and mother had let their house at Foxrock and gone on a trip to New Zealand to see Marjorie. They were to go on from there to Dorothy in Port Elizabeth in South Africa. Since Dorothy's children had begun to grow up she had started painting again and was making quite a name for herself.

If I thought we were coming back to peace and plenty in Ireland

112

I made a great mistake. There may have been plenty but there was no peace. The Black and Tan War was going on, with shooting, curfews, ambushes, murders in the street in broad daylight and every kind of horror. By the time we had found a house there was a truce, and later on the Treaty with England was signed. What was good enough for the Irish leader Michael Collins, however, was not good enough for some of the other patriots. We were soon back where we started, with even worse shooting and murdering. The British had gone and we now had a civil war to face up to.

We moved to Clonard, on the outskirts of Dublin, in 1922, on a Saturday. It was a most attractive small house, with a lodge at the gate where we installed a gardener and his wife. Our gardener's name was Cook and he stayed with us for about thirty years. I remember him saying as we moved in, 'Saturday's flitting is short sitting.' He was right. We had only been there some months when we were burnt out by the Irregulars who were fighting the Cosgrave Government. Gordon was working for the Government, which was executing its opponents, and there were reprisals for the executions; so his name was on the murder list. It was an unnerving time of waiting to be shot or of having your house burnt over your head.

I could not decide which was worse, a night of storm when every banging door or rattling window sounded like men breaking in, or a terribly silent night when the slightest creak might be the approach of an invader. We got little sleep, as we were in constant expectation of a raid.

At last it came—on a wild, stormy night just before Christmas 1922. We were sitting in a little back-room which had steps down to the garden when I heard a noise in the hall. I went out of the room and shut the door behind me, thinking that if it was a raid Gordon could escape by the garden. The hall was filled with masked men with revolvers. I heard myself say, 'Gentlemen, what can we do for you?' The leader came forward very politely and said, 'We have orders to burn this house,' and added, 'We think real bad of doing it. We'll do as little damage as we can. We'll use paraffin. We won't use petrol.' I said, 'There are children here—there must not

113

be any shooting.' They said, 'No, we won't do any shooting.' I was almost beginning to enjoy myself.

Gordon came out of the room and the man again explained their presence and said they would give us time to collect anything we wanted and then we would have to stay in the kitchen downstairs till they got the place alight. They said they would have to cut the phone, but we could get to one next door to ring for the fire brigade. I went to Paddy's room to wake him. He had a boy friend, David Fitzgerald, staying with him who had come up from Greystones because he wanted to hear some shooting; it was too quiet down there. I could not help feeling that I was giving this boy a great thrill when I shook him by the shoulder saying, 'Wake up, David, there are men here to burn the house!'

Gordon appeared carrying Biddy and we all went down to the kitchen, where a man stood guard over us. We could hear the intruders running about upstairs, making bonfires of our bedclothes, and then I suddenly thought of all the Christmas presents behind a screen in my room—the Meccano, the train set, the doll's cot. The idea of having to do the Christmas shopping all over again was too much. I told the guard about the toys and he said, 'Where are they, mum? We'll help you.' He and I ran up the short stairs into the hall. The men there, hearing the running feet, must have thought it was an attack from the rear and I found myself confronted with a dozen revolvers. I held up my hands and said, 'The children's Christmas presents are behind a screen in the end room.'

The place was full of smoke, and already several rooms were alight. Some of the men came with me and helped to collect the toys. It was hard for them to hold on to their revolvers and keep the train-set pieces from falling out of their boxes. We took the toys down to the kitchen and then there was a shout and the raiders left. There were about twenty of them, mostly local men. Our cook met one of them a few days later and he said to her, 'We was all round the house lookin' in through the windows for an hour before we went in. We seen you washin' your feet.'

After the raiders had gone, we took the children down to the lodge and Gordon went to telephone for the fire brigade. I had a feeling that when the fire brigade came it would be like the British

Navy going into action, but it turned out to be more like a performance by the Crazy Gang. First they passed the house and disappeared into the distance. Then they came back and couldn't find the fire hydrant on the road. Then they found that their hoses were too short to get to the house. Then one of them went in by the hall-door; the wind was on the other side of the house, the door banged to and he was nearly smothered by smoke. They had to break down the door to get him out.

I went round to the garden at the back of the house and stood in the wind and the rain in an ecstasy of relief—no one had been shot or burnt. As I watched the flames in the bedroom windows I had a most wonderful moment feeling that everything that I owned was being destroyed. No more possessions—I experienced an extraordinary sense of freedom.

By the time the fire was got under control we found that it had really done comparatively little damage—a few bedrooms burnt out —but that the brigade had reduced every room to a sodden mess. People sent in messages from surrounding houses asking if they could help us. Mrs Cook came to me saying, 'Mr Flanagan wants to know, can he do anything?' I asked who Mr Flanagan was. Mrs Cook replied, 'The undertaker.' His inquiry, I believe, was not made in his professional capacity. We had really been very lucky in having such accommodating raiders. A few nights before our raid three children had been burnt to death and people shot in similar circumstances.

The people next door sent in a message saying that they had beds ready for us and cocoa for the children, and the rest of that night we spent with them, until in the morning my mother-in-law came and took us all to their house. As Gordon's father was now Chairman of the Senate he had a large armed guard at his house, and after one night there we decided that, because of the children and the fear of certain shooting if there was another raid, we must find somewhere else to live. We sent the two maids home, and were fortunate in having good friends who took us in for Christmas. Gordon had to change his place of residence every night, as he was watched and followed so that he could be used as a reprisal for an execution any time he wanted. The children and

I spent a month living in one room in a maternity-home that was owned by a nurse friend of mine. It was a big room with bare boards for the floor, and there was a long horse-hair sofa on castors which the children used as a boat. They propelled themselves round the room by using the fire-irons as oars, and were very happy till the patients underneath us sent up messages to say that the noise was driving them mad.

At night when the children were asleep I would sit at the window of our room and listen to the gun-fire in the city. As there was a curfew at this time the streets would be empty. Sometimes a man came out of a hall-door and stood on the steps or a woman leaned out of a window, just listening, like me. I often thought that the newspapers next morning would have long lists of casualties, but it was extraordinary how few people seemed to get shot in spite of the bombardments and the explosions that went on.

I remember seeing an old, ragged, hump-backed figure of a woman shuffling along on our side of the street one night. She was talking to herself and laughing, and I was curious to know what she was saying. Just as she arrived under my window there came a sudden loud outburst of firing. She paused, looked back in the direction of the sound, then turned on her way again, chuckling and muttering, 'I don't care who they shoot as long as they don't shoot me.'

I find Dublin greatly changed - Sarah Purser is slain by a
postage stamp - Aunt Amelia engages a maid - The strange
behaviour of Sarah Burke - Deathbed of a family retainer -
I happen upon startling revelations - The hey-day of the
Arts Club - Tom Casement of the Life-saving Service -
Romantic notes and rolling smoke - A problem and a
photograph - Succour for a concert party

About a year later we got back to Clonard, and by now the political situation had improved. It was about this time that my father-in-law, who was then Lord Chancellor of Ireland, told us of a beautiful Ward in Chancery that he had in his custody, Denise Daly. He was distressed about her because she wanted to marry 'an elderly, deaf madman in London'. He had not met the man, but this was the description he had been given. We were rather astonished to find that the 'elderly, deaf madman' was the handsome and fabulous Horace de Vere Cole, who had amused and infuriated London for years with his wonderfully worked-out practical jokes.

We once lunched with Horace and Denise, after their marriage, at a Kingstown hotel where they were staying; Joseph Hone and his wife Vera were also there. Horace was in the bath when we arrived and he remained there so long that Denise suggested that we should go up and beat on the door to get him out. We did so. He emerged in silence and began to throw everything that he could find on the landing out of the window which was at the front of the hotel—housemaids' mops, buckets, ornaments, other people's shoes. Denise took it all in laughing good humour. The hotel proprietor was not so amused.

I remember Horace talking of beauty in women and saying the nose was the only feature that really mattered, pointing to Denise's nose as a perfect example. I think Denise had a difficult time with him, but as she was rather a handful herself it probably evened things out.

Dublin was for me a very different place now from the Dublin I had left. My brothers and sisters were scattered. Edna was married and in Vancouver Island, Dorothy in Africa, Marjorie in New Zealand, Philip in India; Malcolm and Ronald had gone to be tobacco-planters in Central Africa. Only Sarah Purser's 'At Home' Day was the same and even that had its differences. The talk would still be on Art and Politics in Ireland but there were new faces round her large drawing-room in Mespil House, and Cosgrave and some of the Ministers had become good friends of hers. She was then nearly ninety years of age, but her interest in everything remained as keen as ever.

Sarah's Stained Glass Works was still turning out windows, and I went back there to do a window for Carrickmines Church in memory of three brothers that we had known who had been killed in the war. It has been said that what really caused Sarah Purser's death was a new stamp that had been issued by the Office of Posts and Telegraphs. It had a portrait on it of her old friend Dr Douglas Hyde, who was then President. Sarah said with some truth that it made him look like 'an old walrus', and was ringing him up to tell him to have it withdrawn when she collapsed. She died a few days later.

My maternal grandmother was another wonderful old lady, and she lived to be well over ninety years of age. While she was still young her husband, a doctor, had died from an illness contracted from one of his patients. It was a struggle to bring up her family but she managed it. Her sons all did well for themselves and her daughters got married, all except my sweet and gentle Aunt Amelia who lived with her mother and cared for her till her death.

Once when my grandmother and Aunt Amelia were without a maid, my aunt found a girl weeping outside their front garden gate. This girl had come up from the country looking for work, and had taken the horse-tram to Kenilworth Square which had its terminus near my grandmother's house; she was completely lost and did not know where to go. My aunt took her in and she remained there for most of the rest of her life.

Her name was Sarah Burke and she became almost an institution in the family. She knew every member of it and all about them and was loved and respected. I remember her as a short, plump, fair-haired, freckled country girl when as a child I used sometimes to stay with my grandmother. After breakfast, when my grandmother read aloud from the Bible, Sarah was sent for and she sat on a chair near the door to join in the prayers. My aunt not only taught her everything she knew about cooking and housework, but even how to read and write.

After my grandmother died my Aunt Amelia lived alone with Sarah. Their house was not very far from Clonard, and I used to go to see them. It was a comfort to feel that so faithful and devoted a retainer was looking after my aunt, but I was rather surprised to notice occasional signs of a change in Sarah's manner and expression. Usually she was very humble, servile and ingratiating, but from time to time she looked at me in a hard and contemptuous way and even spoke slightingly of the family who had been her world for forty years.

One day when I called, Sarah seemed almost hostile and I was surprised to find my aunt in tears and with a faint smell of whiskey about her, a drink which I knew would never be found in that house. Through her tears my aunt said, 'Sarah is so cross with me, she makes me sign things.' I thought she was just wandering in her mind, and as the next time I went Sarah was all smiles and friendliness I put aside my suspicions.

Before my aunt died she seemed very distressed and said to me, 'What is to become of poor Sarah?' I assured her that I would look after her as if she was my own for as long as I lived. A cousin from England came over to settle up my aunt's affairs after her death, and the furniture and things in the house were divided up among the family. A small pension was arranged for Sarah, which I was to pay to her once a month. Sarah found a room for herself and moved into it with furniture which she had been given. I employed her twice a week doing odd jobs and paid her well.

For eleven years I looked after Sarah. In spite of her Old Age Pension and the family pension and my payments, she never seemed to have any money. She was often ill. I brought her food and clothes and even, in the back of my car, coal for her fire. She lived in one small corner of her room with a bed and a chair near the fireplace. The rest of the room was filled with furniture, trunks and boxes, all covered up with sheets of newspaper.

During one of my visits I accidentally moved one of the newspapers. As it slid off on to the ground I was surprised to see a little Chippendale table, on which were some dove-grey Crown Derby cups and saucers. As these things had been looked on as treasures in the family I could not help remarking on their presence to Sarah. She put on her most humble, soapy, servile manner and said, 'Poor Miss Amelia, with her dying breath she said, "Sarah, you are to have the tea-cups and the little table" '

As time went on Sarah spent more and more time in hospital, but she always got back to her room as soon as she could. She kept it locked and padlocked. I often found her very ill but refusing to leave though I had got a bed for her in some hospital. Once I had almost to force her to leave. We had got to her door when she looked back and said, 'Me rosary beads is all in bits.' They were lying in her bed, broken into many pieces. I said, 'If only you'll come I'll get you a new rosary blessed by the Pope!'

When Sarah was safely installed in hospital I rang up a Roman Catholic friend of mine to ask where I could get some rosary beads that had had a Papal blessing. Luckily she knew of a young priest who had lately been in Rome and could supply what I wanted, and he very kindly sent the beads to me on the understanding that if Sarah died they were to be twisted round her fingers.

Sarah was a long time in hospital, and was very popular because of her rosary beads, the whole ward wanting to borrow them. She was later moved to a 'Rest for the Dying' home, where I went to see her. A nun accompanied me to her bedside and we looked down at her. She had had a stroke, and the old face, twisted and queer; she seemed to be asleep. The nun said, 'Speak to her. Tell her who you are.' I leaned tenderly over her and said, 'Sarah, do you know me? It is Miss Beatrice.' One eye slowly opened; it looked at me very coldly, and she said, 'Aye, I know ye.' The eye closed again and we moved away. I told the nun the beads were to be put in her hands if she died.

The Reverend Mother rang me a few days later and told me Sarah was dead, but that the beads were nowhere to be found though everyone had searched for them. After her coffin had been closed down, one of the nurses found the beads hanging from the wire springs under the bed. It was too late to put them in her hands, so they were looped on to the handle of the coffin.

A few days later a big, decent-looking, elderly man called on me, saying that he was Sarah's brother. Before her death she had given him a key and a receipt for an attaché-case which had been lodged in a bank. The bank would not give him the case, and had asked whether there was a Will for Probate. He did not understand this, so he had come to me. As Sarah had left a Will leaving her 'savings' to this brother and her furniture to a niece, I put the matter in the hands of our solicitor and went to him with the key and the receipt. Things had begun to look so suspicious that I asked him to ring me up when he opened the attaché-case. He did so later, and said that he and the Bank Manager were still counting up the lodgements in banks, the Post Office Savings Book Accounts, the Savings Certificates, all the bank-notes and loose cash—it had already come to well over £4,000.

I went with our solicitor to Sarah's room, and threw aside all the newspapers. There were boxes and boxes of bits of soap, pairs of scissors, trunks full of knitting wool and Paddy's typewriting-paper, as well as endless small objects and things from my grandmother's house which Sarah had no right to. I was so indignant that I said to the solicitor, 'Everything in this room is mine.' He laughed and asked me if I was prepared to go into a Court of Law and prove it. That seemed too difficult, so I did nothing; but I had the satisfaction of telling the hospitals (which had treated Sarah free of charge because of her poverty) to send in their bills, and saw that the Little Sisters of the Poor had a cheque because of their care of her, and also the pleasant woman in whose house Sarah had been a lodger.

For years a rich niece of my aunt, who was a bit vague about dealing with money matters, had been sending her money from England to give comfort to her old age. Sarah had been cashing these cheques and lodging them to her own account. She must have saved every penny she ever earned in her forty years with my grandmother and aunt as well as the money I paid her while she worked for me. I thought of the rosary beads which had refused to be twined in Sarah's unrepentant thieving hands and the, 'Aye, I know ye,' which really meant, 'Of all the silly, unsuspecting, gullible fools that I ever had to deal with, you were the silliest.'

In Dublin the Arts Club was in its hey-day. Its members now included W. B. Yeats and his wife, Georgie, also his brother Jack. There were playwrights, poets, painters, writers, lawyers and politicians and many clever or odd people either connected with the arts or with some personal quality of their own. It was amazing how much talent and originality went into the ballads, songs, and other performances specially written for the club dinners. Cruise O'Brien and his sister would go behind a screen and we would hear a discussion, apparently between Lady Gregory and W. B. Yeats, about the Abbey Theatre; or Sir Horace Plunkett and Father Dineen giving their opinions on the revival of the Irish language. The scripts were as clever as the mimicry of the voices.

We also performed little plays and had dances, play-readings and discussions. Kot had given me a Russian blouse, which came in very useful for Tchekov. How lovely and how Russian Ria Mooney looked in it, with her smooth black hair and her slightly Slavonic face! Jack Yeats was one of our most amusing and original after-dinner speakers. He once made a speech in French, though he confessed that he did not know a word of the language; it sounded very convincing, and it was all about the taking of the Bastille!

In the early 'twenties Tom Casement made his appearance. He got a room in the Arts Club and soon became one of its oddest and most amusing members. He was a younger brother of Sir Roger Casement, whom he always spoke of as 'Roddy'. As a boy he had gone to sea as an apprentice in a sailing-ship in the Australian trade, and when his time on the half-deck had expired he took his various 'tickets' and became an officer. After some years he 'swallowed the anchor' and 'took to the beach' in Africa, where he tried his hand at many things.

For some time Tom was British Consul in Delagoa Bay, in Portuguese East Africa. He fought in the Boer War and in the First World War, in which he held the rank of Captain and was a personal friend of General Smuts. He was a wonderful spinner of yarns and held us entranced with his stories of life on sailing-ships or digging for diamonds in Johannesburg. On arrival in Dublin he went to Gordon at the Ministry of Industry with the idea of creating a Coast Life-saving Service round Ireland (after the departure of the British, the Coastguard Stations had fallen into disuse). Gordon got the proposal adopted and Tom played his part very well.

Gordon was so impressed by the unusualness of Tom Casement that he brought him out to Clonard, and almost from our first meeting Tom attached himself to me like a very faithful and devoted dog. He had no idea of what his age was and he might have been anything from thirty to seventy. He was tall and had some resemblance to his brother Roger, but without the beard. Tom dressed in Irish tweeds with a double-breasted coat and a tweed hat, and took a pride in his appearance, knowing that he always looked distinctive and original. He was quite incapable of keeping his money.

I happened to mention that I was interested in models of sailing-ships in bottles. Tom searched Dublin and went to auctions till our house was filled with such things. He had his haunts in the hostelries of Dublin, of which the 'Scotch House' was his favourite. He collected an extraordinary set of odd characters round him as drinking companions, who might all have come out of Joyce's *Ulysses*. He backed bills for them, and paid the nursing-home fees when their wives were having babies.

Tom had his head office or store for the life-saving equipment in a sort of stone cellar with barred windows in Fleet Street, which had once been the cells of the College Street Police Station. His second-in-command was a grand old seafaring man named Captain Foster, who looked after Tom as if he was a child.

One day I called to see Tom; he was out, and Captain Foster said furiously, in a voice like a ship's fog-horn, 'It is his pay-day; he has gone out to find someone to lend money to.' He used to write romantic little notes to me saying, 'You are the greatest thing in my life since Roddy.' Alan Duncan's wife in the Arts Club happened to mention to me that she had had 'such a touching little note' from Tom saying she was 'the greatest thing in his life since

Roddy'. Interested in this aspect of Tom, we went round the club making inquiries. Every sort of woman, old or young, fat or thin, had been the greatest thing in Tom's life since Roddy.

While I was on the House Committee in the club, I found a fearful lot of rubbish in all kinds of holes and corners. I got Tom to help me to collect this and put it out in a small back-yard till I made arrangements for it to be removed by the Corporation refuse carts. There were old carpets, rugs, bits of linoleum, broken furniture and every sort of junk. After my day's labour I went home.

Next day I heard that after I had gone Tom had had the brilliant idea of setting fire to the whole heap. Volumes of black, reeking smoke billowed up into the windows of the surrounding houses; inky clouds swept through the Arts Club and out through the hall-door into Lower Fitzwilliam Street. The doctors were being suffo-cated in their consulting-rooms. The fire brigade was sent for. The police were sent for. The President of the Royal Hibernian Academy was sent for. When Tom saw the full horror of the situation which he had created he hurried off to the 'Scotch House' to hide himself among his cronies. He was so naïve and charming that no one ever held anything against him.

Tom was a very keen follower of Rugby football. He went the rounds of Twickenham, Murrayfield, Cardiff and Lansdowne Road every year for the International matches, wearing pyjamas under his suit to avoid carrying any luggage. His most serious problem was where to put his money. At one great jubilation over a win for Ireland at Cardiff he had 'passed out'. On coming to next day he found that his wallet with his money and his ticket back to Dublin had gone. We had great discussions about where I could sew his money on to him but he decided he would be in a worse fix if he was unable to find it when he wanted it.

At one time in his life Tom had been married, in Africa; he showed me a photograph of his wife. He called her 'Blanche'. The marriage did not last long. They tried to run a hotel on Kiliman-jaro, but had no water and Tom apparently spent all his time taking pretty girls on the backs of mules up to the summit of the moun-tain to see the sunrise or the sunset. Blanche, who was a painter, decided to go back to her painting, so their partnership came to an end.

Tom came with us to the West of Ireland several times. We hired a sailing-boat at Mallaranny, which led to a lot of idiotic adventures. Tom's heart was in boats and sailing-ships. He used to sing sea-shanties and he taught the children how to make Turk's Heads. He was always wanting to help the 'down-and-outs' and usually got me involved in his schemes.

On Achill Island he found a stranded, penniless London concert party consisting of two men, three women and a couple of banjoes. The people on the island could not understand their language. Perceiving that it was a hopeless place to have come to, the party only wanted to get back to London; they were by now almost starving. To try to help these people Tom had the great idea of buying an alarm-clock and making a lot of numbered tickets, which we sold as raffle tickets for a few pence. He tried to explain his plan to his audience, holding up the alarm-clock. He then drew the winning ticket and the woman with the same number got the clock. When all the other red-petticoated and homespun members of the crowd saw that they were to get nothing they surged angrily forward demanding clocks. We had either to give them back their money or try to find another couple of dozen alarm-clocks. We gave back the money.

Then Tom suggested that we should arrange a concert for the Londoners in the hotel at Mallaranny where we were staying. I was doubtful about how this would work. The people in the hotel were all rather superior and prosperous-looking, with big cars. Anyhow, Tom insisted. We got permission from the management, filled the big drawing-room with chairs and put up posters. We were not allowed to charge for admission but could take a collection. Screens were arranged at the end of the room as dressing-rooms. Our mummers arrived shaking with terror. Tom also had begun to lose his nerve and to fortify himself he had been having rather too many 'snifters'.

Anyway, the mummers did their turns, little cockney songs with banjo accompaniment, a little dance, even a little play. The on-lookers seemed delighted. When the show was finished one of the

most distinguished members of the audience, an elderly gentleman, stood up and made a touching little speech about the concert
party's predicament. He then headed the collection with a generous
contribution, everyone else following suit. I remember the poor
thin painted faces of the women with tears of gratitude in their
eyes. Tom was weeping too.

*Ballads and bathing with George Bernard Shaw - Views and
influence of a dramatist - I become a mother again - Souvenirs
of Irish-American friendship - Death of my mother - My
husband writes a play - Tom Casement in leopard-skins and
straitened circumstances - Sharks, seagulls and Bob Flaherty -
A refusal and a re-encounter - John Hughes savours an
old oath - Winter in Switzerland - Death of a Life-Saver - I
battle against a blizzard - Return to gentler climes*

It was shortly after we had moved back to Clonard that we spent
a few weeks at Parknasilla, in Kerry. Bernard Shaw and Mrs Shaw
were also staying in the hotel. They had a private sitting-room,
where Shaw was writing *St Joan*. Both were very friendly with the
other visitors and Shaw was popular with the children, who looked
on him as a nice elderly gentleman very interested in cameras.

We had a car and we used to take them for long drives over
the mountains. We passed many places showing signs of the
'Troubles': blown-up bridges, burnt-out houses and the remains of
ambushes on the roads. Shaw was very interested in the street-
ballads that had come out of those times. I remember we were
all out in a boat on the Kenmare river, with Shaw rowing, when
he asked us about them. We sang:

> In Mountjoy Gaol on Monday morning
> High upon the gallows tree
> Kevin Barry gave his young life
> For the cause of liberty.
> Another martyr for Old Ireland,
> Another murder for the Crown,
> Cruel laws to crush the Irish
> For to break their spirits down.

He liked the comic ones best and sang with us, to the tune
'Yankee Doodle':

de Valera had a cat
Who sat upon the fender,
Every time she heard a shot
She shouted 'No surrender'.

Kot had often spoken of Shaw as 'that old music-hall entertainer', though he would add 'he made himself into a great journalist'. I could not help remembering Kot's phrase one day at the bathing-place when Shaw took the lifebelt that hung there and gave us a demonstration in the sea of how dangerous a thing it was, showing us all the different ways it could trap you and drown you. At times it seemed as if the lifebelt had really got the better of Shaw. With his two feet sticking up through it, it seemed unlikely that his head would ever appear again. There was a lot of laughter, but Mrs Shaw looked really quite anxious.

Mrs Shaw was one of the gentlest, kindest people I ever met and she seemed to like us as much as we liked her. She sent us each a separate Christmas card every year from then up to her death. She loved Ireland and everything about it, and always seemed hurt when G.B.S. mocked at it and derided it. She came to me one day and asked, 'Is your husband English?', saying G.B.S. had decided he was. I said, 'No', and told her that Gordon was 'born and bred in the City of Dublin'. G.B.S. came up at that moment and I asked him why he thought Gordon was English. He replied, 'He seemed to be a person of some education and intelligence, so I naturally concluded he was English.'

I once asked Shaw why he never came to Dublin. He replied, 'What has Dublin got that I should go there?' I could not think of anything, but said, 'Good talk.' Shaw said, 'Who talks in Dublin?' Hesitatingly I said, 'Oliver Gogarty.' He snorted, 'Silly Dublin persiflage!'

It is almost impossible for young people today to realize what Shaw meant to my generation. The excitement, the shock of having all one's deeply-rooted conventions blown to pieces, the revelation of a new way of thought, a new attitude towards women, towards everything. Shaw seemed pleased by my description of coming out of a theatre, after one of his plays, liberated and

George Bernard Shaw, Parknasilla, 1922

Gordon Campbell with Mr and Mrs G. B. Shaw, Co. Kerry

John Hughes, from a water-colour
drawing by Walter Osborne.
Behind him is his marble group
'Orpheus and Euridice' now in
the Dublin Municipal Gallery
(*by courtesy of the National
Gallery of Ireland*)

John Hughes in the
Modelling Room, 1900

exhilarated. Kot used to say that Shaw never said anything new, he was only the mouthpiece of what was in the air at that time. These liberating ideas may have been in the air in London, but they certainly had not got as far as Foxrock in County Dublin.

My younger son Michael was born in 1924. It was lovely to have a baby in the house again. George Moore once said, 'The body has no memories.' This may explain the fact that in looking back now I feel that having a baby was great fun and a great adventure.

It was in the early hours of 25 October that I left Clonard in a taxi to go to the nursing-home. I was to call for my nurse at her house on the way. There I sat in the taxi waiting for her; it was a still dark night. The clock in the tower of the Town Hall at Rathmines struck four, every stroke of the bell sounding strong and beautiful in the silent empty street. All my senses seemed more acute and awake than usual. In the home, two nurses were making my bed; their white clothes and the white sheets were snowier than anything I had ever seen, and the electric light extraordinarily bright.

As I stood in my bare feet on a white fur rug in front of a radiant fire, I saw my face in a glass over the fireplace. There was such a beaming smile on it I had to turn away to hide it. I was afraid the nurses might think I was mad. By midday I was not feeling so splendid. My doctor, Bethel Solomons, came—and how grateful I was for the sweet sickly smell of chloroform; deep breaths of it while the doctor's and nurses' voices drifted farther and farther away.

After seemingly years of oblivion I heard Bethel's voice again, saying, 'Wake up and see what a lovely boy you have.' Then that wonderful moment of terrible tenderness like nothing else in life, when the little warm bundle is laid beside you and you feel the touch of the downy head on your cheek.

There is some unique quality in a maternity-home. While one is a patient there it seems the very centre and core of existence. Men hardly exist, even the doctor is almost an intruder. The outside world with its wars and all it works seems so much nonsense. The talk, the jokes, the babies and the flowers! The maternity-home becomes a small world of tremendous importance, full of deep mother-and-child peace.

The woman who ran the home I was in had given up nursing and kept a few Pekinese dogs instead. She was rather a character. Last thing at night she used to take her dogs out for a walk and during the curfew years she completely ignored the regulations. Once when she was outside her house with her dogs after curfew, a lorry-load of Black and Tans came roaring down the street; one of them yelled at her, 'Get in to Hell out of that!' She was furious at her home being called 'Hell'.

When the British Army first went to South Africa to fight the Boers they wore red coats and helmets which could be seen helio-graphing for miles in the sunshine, but they soon decided that it would be safer to blend more with the colour of the bushveld. In Ireland at that time there was a good deal of sympathy for the 'Boorjers' (as they were affectionately called) who had been res-ponsible for this change of costume, and now when the Black and Tans drove about in their weird lorries it was said that 'it took the Boorjers to put the British Army in khaki, but it took the Irish to put them in cages'.

When Michael was a few months old Gordon went to America with an Irish delegation to a World Parliamentary Congress. His presence in the delegation was explained by a scheme he was working on for the Government, which was to harness the Shannon and supply Ireland with electricity. The German firm of Siemens-Schuckert was to carry out this work and Gordon was to make inquiries about electrical development in the U.S.A.

As it was the first time that representatives of an Irish Govern-ment had visited America the whole trip turned into a round of splendid parties sponsored by Irish-American millionaires. The Irish visitors were feasted and fêted. They drove through the streets with motor-cycle escorts, all the sirens wailing. They had their pro-grammes at baseball matches signed by Babe Ruth and other national heroes. Gordon had always disliked travelling—he hated 'abroad'—but America was different. All the women were beauti-ful, and they all wept when he read Yeats's poems aloud to them.

Among his souvenirs of the trip were several small lace hand-kerchiefs which had been drenched with tears.

My father and mother had enjoyed their trip to New Zealand and to South Africa so much that in 1925 they decided to go again. To my mother it was all an enthralling adventure. I remember my father telling me about a storm in the Bay of Biscay and how they laughed when all the furniture in the lounge started sweeping backwards and forwards with the roll of the ship, and how funny it was when my mother was swept across the floor in her chair and hit her head against the piano. I gathered that my mother laughed too. I always thought that my father had some resemblance to Mr Pooter in *The Diary of a Nobody*. When he told me the story I could imagine Mr Pooter saying, 'Lord, how we roared!'

On their second trip my parents went to Nyasaland, where my brother Malcolm was married and had become a tobacco-planter with land of his own. Ronald had been with him for a while but had died there from tuberculosis, which he contracted during the East African Campaign in the First World War, when the South African Scottish were left in their summer outfits through the rainy season and cold nights as their commissariat was all bogged down in the floods of the Zambesi, hundreds of miles away.

The heat and the altitude were too much for my mother, who was well over seventy at this time. She became ill there and died at Grahamstown on her way back to Dorothy at Port Eliza-beth. It was just as she would have liked it; she always longed to travel, it was all part of her Great Adventure. My father returned home and finally went to live with Philip and his wife in England after Philip had retired from the R.A.M.C., with a D.S.O. and an M.C.

In 1928 Gordon wrote a charming and witty play, which was produced by Shelah Richards at the Peacock Theatre for one night with Ralph Brereton-Barry in the principal part. As the name of the play was *Treaty with the Barbarians* there was a gathering of the politically minded ladies of Dublin, headed by Madame Maud Gonne McBride in the front row, probably hoping that they would be exhorted to uphold the cause of Ireland. The play had no politics in it, however, and went off very pleasantly. Jack Yeats told

Gordon that he had a 'money-spinner'; but it never went any farther or spun any money.

Tom Casement always came to me to make up a costume for him for the Nine Arts Fancy Dress Ball, which was a great affair rather on the lines of the one in Chelsea. He was very pleased with his appearance one year when I made him up as a pirate. After one of his expeditions to auction-rooms to search out model ships for me he brought back a large Kaffir shield, some leopard-skins, spears, assegais and knobkerries. I had no idea what to do with them, but when the time for the Nine Arts Ball arrived I was visited by the inspiration to make Tom up as a Zulu chief. He was a very modest man and insisted on wearing brown woollen underclothes beneath his leopard-skins with only his face, hands and feet showing, and even his warrior's feet were covered with shoes.

As he had no way of finding out his correct age, Tom kept on his Civil Service post till long after the time when he should have retired. When he finally had to give it up he was almost penniless as there was no pension attached. His very kind cousin, Mary Parry of Cushenden, paid for his board and lodging, and for pocket-money I got up a subscription and gave him some of the proceeds every week. This was humiliating for him, but there was no other way. It was very difficult to make him claim his Old Age Pension, for he still felt he was only twenty-five. He was quite bewildered and hurt by the attitude of some of his one-time friends. He told me how before he had given up his job men used to gather round him when he went into the 'Scotch House', but now they all seemed to slip away or have other engagements.

Michael was still a small boy when he and I went with the playwright Denis Johnston and his actress wife Shelah Richards to the Aran Islands, where Bob Flaherty was shooting *Man of Aran*. It was very exciting and interesting, with huge basking sharks harpooned and towed into the little harbour. I remember Flaherty trying to get a shot of masses of seagulls in flight. They were all so gorged with basking shark that nothing would make them rise from the surface of the water. The people of the islands looked on Flaherty as a god and were all ready to fling themselves into any kind of danger, even death itself, for the sake of the film, the making of which was the most wonderful thing that had ever happened to them.

I think it was Denis Johnston who brought Ninette de Valois to Clonard on one of her visits to her native land. Michael was then about nine years old; she looked at him and said, 'Give me that boy, he is the right build and appearance. I can make a dancer of him', but Michael did not want to become a dancer, his interests at that time were all in motor races and racing cars.

After Michael had gone to his preparatory boarding school I went to Paris for a short time to play at being an art student again. I went every day to draw at Colorossie's. I had not seen John Hughes for many years, when he came to my hotel. He seemed much older and smaller and more like a Frenchman than ever, and he wore a beret. He must have seen my thoughts in my face, for he said, 'Am I different?' I said, 'You have no moustache.' He said, 'It was the war. I had either to lose a leg or my moustache, I chose my moustache.'

Hughes said he had almost given up sculpture, he was playing the flute instead. I remembered how he used to whistle things from Gluck's *Orfeo* in the modelling-room with a quality of sound just like a flute. He still lived with a sister to whom he was devoted, and he did not wish me to go to their flat. I felt they were in poor circumstances.

We met every afternoon and sat outside cafés and walked in the Luxembourg Gardens. He showed me a statue there that he loved, somewhere near the one of George Sand. It is of some sort of a druidess and seems to have no name; he never could find out who did it. We talked endlessly about the old School of Art and the modelling-room where he used to read aloud to us. Sometimes it was Dante's *Inferno* in Italian; we liked the sound of it but none of us understood a word. Another time it was *The Hound of the Baskervilles* and we were all so thrilled we forgot to model and the model forgot to pose; we all gathered round him to listen and he was as excited as we were. We went to the Louvre and found that we both loved the Ingres portraits and the wonderful 'Bathsheba' by Rembrandt, with her little pensive face, the letter in her hand and the old woman washing her feet. It was a great happiness to look at pictures together, we were so much in sympathy.

Hughes asked about everyone that he had ever known in Dublin, including a charming young woman, Miss Betty Webb, who had been Sir Thornly Stoker's secretary. I told him that I had not seen or heard of her for years, and that the last time I had seen her was at the opening, by the Lord Mayor, of some loan exhibition of pictures. Betty Webb was standing beside me when the Lord Mayor began his speech, in a terribly broad, flat Dublin accent. She turned to me and said softly, 'Be th' hokey fly!'

When I told this to John Hughes, I thought I saw a queer look come over his face. He came nearer to me and said, 'Would you say that again?' I repeated it very carefully. He turned and walked away, and I saw him take out his handkerchief. He sat on a seat, held his handkerchief to his eyes, and seemed shaken with sobs. I thought I had done something awful to him, broken his heart perhaps. I went to sit beside him, then saw he was helpless with laughter. He said, 'I haven't heard that expression for sixty years. It is marvellous!' He repeated it, savouring its quality and enjoying it. When he met me next day he told me how he woke in the night and thought of it. He had laughed out loud, and his sister had knocked on the partition between their rooms to ask him what was the matter.

John Hughes loved beauty. I remember a sort of little office he had in the corner of the modelling-room. He came out of it one day wiping tears from his eyes and said, 'I have been reading *Romeo and Juliet*. Their conversation is so beautiful it has made me cry.' A few years after I had met him again in Paris his sister died. He wrote to me saying, 'Don't try to comfort me.' He left Paris, I think he went to Italy, and I never heard of him again.

After Michael left his prep school with a scholarship to St Columba's College, he had pleurisy. As it was the beginning of the winter months his doctor thought it would be wise for him to recuperate in some place where there was sunshine, so he and I went to Arosa in Switzerland. It was beautiful there, but there was very little to do, as we were not winter-sporting. Michael got some amusement out of a *luge* and I did a lot of reading.

One of our amusements was to go to the little railway station in the afternoon to meet the train and buy the Continental *Daily Mail*. The woman in the newspaper-stall was very friendly and made a point of finding out the names of her clients, but she did not always manage to get them quite correct. She once addressed me very cheerfully as 'Lady Godiva': I saw Michael disappear round the corner of the stall to hide his laughter. I had had letters from Tom Casement, who had not been well, which said he was counting the days till our return. One afternoon we opened our newspaper and read the tragic news that a brother of Sir Roger Casement had been found drowned in the Grand Canal in Dublin.

Poor Tom, he had been in bed for a few days, but, feeling better, he must have decided to get up and visit some of his old haunts. He had been living in lodgings near the canal, and if he could avoid it he never used the bridge to cross over by, which he said was only for 'landlubbers'. There was a narrow foot-bridge at the head of the lock gates when they were shut, with a handrail, which he used instead. He must have been walking on this, missed his step and slipped down into the deep water. It probably happened on his way home.

When we got back to Dublin, Mr Smyllie, the editor of the *Irish Times* (a very good friend of Tom's), told me of his funeral and the crowds who went to it. There was not enough money for a tombstone, so I got up a subscription, all the men of the Coast Life-saving Service subscribing (they all loved him) and all kinds of unexpected people, even General Smuts. I got someone to do elegant Roman lettering on the stone and modelled a little ship in full sail which was carved on it. I sent a photograph of the grave and the headstone to all stations round the coast where the breeches-buoy apparatus was stored, and received many grateful letters from Tom's men.

Among my memories of that winter in Arosa is the little lending library, with its very English lady-librarian, which was in the crypt of the English Church. It was like a club where the English residents met and talked. Michael and I went there for books. A blizzard was blowing one day as I prepared for my usual trip to the library. The hall-porter at our hotel stared at me in amazement and said, 'You are mad! No one goes out on such a day!' I thought it was no worse than some weather I had seen in Ireland, so set out undaunted.

After a few minutes I realized how extraordinary a real blizzard can be. My face was completely numb, I was solid with snow, and had recollections of the 'very gallant gentleman'. but I just could not turn back to face that hotel porter and admit defeat. There was not a soul to be seen anywhere, and I began to think the library would be snowed up and no one there. Eventually I arrived —there they all were, beating the snow off each other, chatting brightly, completely ignoring the weather; just being 'mad dogs and Englishmen'.

Biddy came out to spend Christmas with us, and we went to some very thrilling ice-hockey matches. It was interesting when a German team came on to the ice and lined up to give the Nazi salute and shout 'Heil Hitler!'—a terrible silence suddenly came over the entire audience, a sort of gloom. As there were other young people from Dublin in the hotel, Biddy got some skiing. It was lovely to have her there and she was company for Michael; he and I had been very much alone. One night I left them together and went to a Bach concert in a Lutheran church in the village. It was most impressive. I looked round at the congregation, working people in poor but clean and tidy clothes, all absorbed in the music.

On Christmas morning we went to the English Church. The young rector was a great admirer of the Reverend Dick Sheppard, and rather copied his ways. He called out from the chancel rail, 'Come in, come in, there is plenty of room.' We started off with 'Oh come, all ye faithful', but the harmonium had just been tuned and the pitch was so high that we might have been struggling through the last movement of the Ninth Symphony, with our vocal cords in agony. It was only by singing everything an octave lower that we managed to get through the remainder of the musical part of the service.

The snow was beginning to melt when the time came for us to

leave Arosa. We were walking together one day when Michael suddenly dashed at a piece of ground under a fir tree, calling out, 'Clay, clay!' I dashed at it too and together we dug and scratched at the lovely brown earth.

On a marvellous spring day, all sunshine and birds singing and flowers everywhere, we arrived back at Clonard. The house seemed completely empty, with the hall-door, the garden-door and all the windows wide open. Biddy's two dogs appeared and looked at us for a second in stunned surprise; then they started to leap straight up into the air on all fours, simply screaming with joy. It was a perfect welcome.

The first time I saw Kot in London after our return from Switzerland, I told him that I had read *War and Peace* while I was there and how wonderful I had found the warm rich life of the book, compared to our hotel rooms and being among strangers and surrounded by those terrible great white mountains. I felt, I said, 'homesick for Russia'. Kot replied, rather scathingly, 'You were not homesick for Russia, you were homesick for Tolstoy. Tolstoy knew everything about every sort of situation and every kind of person—everywhere.'

There is something about Ireland which makes it a lovely place to come back to, the tempo is so slow. The softness of the air and the softness of the water which comes out of the taps, even the softness of the people's voices, are like a caress. Charles Stewart Parnell's sister Annie, who had been at the Dublin School of Art with my mother and my Aunt Annie and had often stayed with them in my grandfather's house in Kilternan, wrote a poem which Joe Hone said was the greatest Irish patriotic poem ever written. It begins:

> Shall mine eyes behold thy glory, O my country?
> Shall mine eyes behold thy glory?
> Or shall the darkness close around them, ere
> The sun-blaze break at last upon thy story?

The poem goes on to tell of the time when Ireland will have achieved its nationhood:

> Ah! the harpings and the salvoes and the shoutings
> of the exiled sons returning!
> *I* shall hear, tho' dead and mouldered, and the
> grave-damp should not chill my bosom's burning.

It might be almost comic, were it not so tragic, that after over thirty-five years of Home Rule and Independence, there is no sound of 'the salvoes and the shoutings of the exiled sons returning'. On the contrary, the sons are still going away in increasing numbers.

13

*Communications from the Lawrences - An exhibition and a
prosecution - Paul Robeson makes us look 'white trash' - I
prove unsatisfactory as a fallen woman - Music in the night -
My daughter completes my education - Dublin parties and
distinguished people - I paint an 'obscene' picture*

We lost touch with Katherine and Murry after our return to Ireland
and only had news of them from Kot. I had kept my promise to
him to go to London once a year to see him and Gertler. He also
used to tell me of Lawrence's and Frieda's travels about the world.
In October 1927 we received the following letter from Lawrence
from the Villa Mirenda, near Florence.

Dear Gordon and Beatrice,

Here's a voice from the past! But Kot said Beatrice was in
London: and somehow I've been thinking about Ireland lately.
(Does Gordon still say 'Ahrland' with gallons of tears in his
voice?)

We've just got back from Germany—and I've a suspicion that
I'm really rather bored by Italy and the Italians; and I have an
idea that next year I should like to try the wild Irish. Should I,
do you think? Do you think Frieda and I should like to spend
a year in Ireland—rent a little furnished house somewhere
romantic, roaring billows and brown bogs sort of thing? Do you
think we should? And is it feasible, practical and all that?
Somewhere where the rain leaves off occasionally. Of course
Ireland is to my mind something like the bottom of an aquarium
with little people in crannies like prawns. But I've got a sort of
hunch about it, that it might mean something to me more than
this Tuscany. It would be great fun to see you both again
especially in native setting. Do you still keep up with Murry?
He's licked all the gum off me, I'm no longer adhesive. I'm serious
about Ireland next year. So write and stop me if I ought to be

stopped. Meanwhile all sorts of greetings, *tante belle cose* from us both, and be sure and send a line in answer!

Yours,

D. H. Lawrence.

It was difficult to know how to advise them or where to get the sort of place that they would like. It certainly was a responsibility, the climate might be the worst possible one for Lawrence's health. After he had got Gordon's reply, he wrote again:

Dear Campbell and Beatrice,

Many thanks for the letter, cautious but encouraging. Was I a monster of impatience? Whether I still am, I don't know. I think I'm a very much sadder and wiser man but I can still see you pulling long faces at me. No, but I'm impatient. We've had this house nearly two years. I really think if we don't go to America to the ranch, we'll come to Ireland—about April. But I get so sick of Europe altogether (impatient too) that I feel I *must* go to America for an antidote. For America *is* somehow an antidote, so tonicky, and one *can't* be weighed down with problems there, one doesn't care. Then there's the ranch—the horses to ride—the space and the freedom. But, of course, America is rough and anarchic and soulless—but not as mercenary as Italy. I should like to see you again—and Beatrice—and hear your melodious voice like a sort of bagpipe. I wish we could come in this evening—you could drone and I could flourish and the women would come in like kettle-drums—wouldn't it be fun? I'd love to have a bit of fun again in the Selwood Terrace and Bucks' style—but there is a certain melancholy, Gordon in a silk hat, but a bathrobe first, with Mrs Conybear singing in the basement—What was it she sang? 'Scenes that are brightest' that Ireland knoweth not, nor politics either.

I think, you know, most probably we'll come. Won't you dread it! Never mind, Beatrice can handle us. Dear Beatrice do please write us some news, he can't.

D. H. Lawrence.

They did not come. Lawrence had turned his attention to the project of publishing *Lady Chatterley* privately in Florence. In a letter from Switzerland in February 1928, he wrote: 'I've got on my conscience a novel I wrote, and which is much too shocking—verbally—for any publisher. Says shit! and fuck! in so many syllables . . . it's a good novel—love, as usual—and very nice too, but says all the things it shouldn't say.' And to Gordon from Florence, March, 1928: 'I'm having it printed in Florence, in a little printer's shop where nobody understands a word of English, so nobody will be able to raise a blush. Isn't that nice! Imagine if the serpent in Paradise had whispered in Gaelic to Eve, when she only understood ancient Hebrew, what a lot of fuss might have been saved.' He had also been painting pictures and Lady Ottoline's niece, Dorothy Warren, was planning to have an exhibition of them in her gallery in London. In the same letter Lawrence wrote:

Did you know I painted pictures, last year—seven or eight big oils, nudes—some people very shocked—worse than my writing. But I think they are rather lovely and almost holy. Are there three children? Somehow I only had track of Biddy and Paddy; and now jazzers and golfers. '*Dio mio!*' Is your hair still the same colour? F. is a bit grey, and I found two white hairs in my beard—I'd really like to come to Ireland, and see you all, and Liam O'Flaherty—and Dublin—and go to the West, I hope it wouldn't always rain.

That was the last we heard about their idea of coming to Ireland. I was in London in 1927 just after the exhibition of Lawrence's pictures had been closed by the police, who had removed thirteen of them, but I managed to see what was left. What to expect I did not know, something strange perhaps and almost frightening, something like Blake; but apart from the subject matter the pictures were almost ordinary. Nothing that Lawrence did could be negligible but they lacked the strange quality that one might have looked for in paintings by such an unusual person.

Gertler and I talked about the exhibition in the Café Royal. We were sad for Lawrence. The news of the reception of his work had driven him into a frenzy of rage and indignation. Such words as 'obscenity', 'pornography' and 'filth' had been used about his 'sincere utterance'. His treatment of sex, nudity and natural functions with a sort of sunny innocence had been too much for the British people. Before the show closed there had been 13,000 visitors at the gallery.

When the case came before the Magistrate, St John Hutchinson was the defending counsel. Though his defence was most convincing, it was no use. He finally had to agree to have the pictures withdrawn with an assurance that they would not be shown again. This was because Lawrence was afraid that they would be burnt if the law took its course. Lawrence had written to Dorothy Warren saying, 'There is something sacred about my pictures, I will not have them burned.'

Shelah Richards's family and my in-laws had known each other and been summer residents in Greystones long before I met any of them. During the war years we used to take a small furnished house there opposite the Richards's. Shelah was then a young girl just leaving school, and her little nephews and nieces, including Geraldine Fitzgerald and her brother David, used to play with my children. I was interested in Shelah, she was so keen to become an actress, and I think it was I who sent her to Lennox Robinson at the Abbey Theatre. He gave her some small parts and although Lady Gregory did not think she was sufficiently 'peasant-stock' for her idea of a National Theatre, Shelah managed to surmount this difficulty and make her mark.

After her marriage to Denis Johnston, while she was on tour with the Abbey Company in America, she met Paul Robeson. It must have been early in the 'thirties when he came to Dublin to give a concert in the old Theatre Royal. The house was packed. To accommodate the overflow they had a great many chairs on the huge stage behind the performers. After the concert Shelah and Denis brought Paul Robeson out to our house. He expressed pleasure at the terrific reception he had received. The concert had begun with a piano solo neither very interesting nor important, and I said I was amazed at the spellbound silence of the Dublin audience during the performance of this item—I was trying to

142

suggest that it was due to the awe-inspiring thought of Paul Robeson's presence behind the scenes. Biddy, a student at Trinity College at this time, said that the reason for the silence was that everyone in the huge auditorium was trying to figure out how many people had been fitted on to the stage. They were counting the people in the front row and then how many rows there were and multiplying one by the other; everyone was arriving at a different solution of the problem. Paul Robeson was much amused at this idea.

One night we took Robeson to the Abbey Theatre. I have never seen such a superb performance of *The Plough and the Stars*. Shelah had passed the word round behind the scenes that Paul Robeson was in front. He was immensely interested and excited by the performance, and we went round to the green-room afterwards where all the actors were still in their tenement-house make-up. They all looked so small, almost invisible beside the huge, splendid, black presence of Robeson. He began to speak to them about what he wanted to do with his own people in his own country. He wanted to create a theatre like the Abbey where primitive speech could be heard in all its beauty; he said it was like singing. To explain this point he went on talking and beating his great black hands together to mark the rhythm. The Abbey actors stood round almost worshipping, gasping, 'God! Isn't he gorgeous!' Robeson certainly did make us all look like 'white trash'.

In those days the Abbey had a very good orchestra, under the direction of Dr Larchet, and during one of the intervals they played an arrangement of Brahms's *Feldeinsamkeit*. As it ended I turned to Robeson and found myself saying the same thing as he was saying to me: 'That is one of the most beautiful songs ever written.'

A new society had been formed in Dublin calling itself the Drama League. We produced and acted plays in the Abbey Theatre on Sunday nights. It was fun painting our own scenery, though the Abbey scene-painter, Seaghan Barlow, very much resented us using his scene-painting room. Some of the painters left it in an awful mess. I became almost popular with Seaghan because I washed the brushes, swept the floor and left everything tidy when

I had finished. We produced many plays, among them a translation of *The Kingdom of God* by Sierra.

In this I played one of the inmates of a home for fallen women. On one of Alice's visits from Spain she had brought me some shawls and a mantilla, and I thought this was a great opportunity to make myself up as a staggering blonde Spanish beauty. When I appeared on the stage for the dress-rehearsal Lennox Robinson, who was producing the play, stared at me in amazement and said, 'What on earth are you dressed up like that for?' I said, 'I am a fallen woman.' He said, 'Go back at once and take off that stuff and get an old black shawl and some shabby clothes from the wardrobe-room and dirty your face and toss your hair.' I began to protest feebly. A funny little scene-shifter was standing near; he was such an odd shape that he was known as 'The Crocodile'. He looked at me sadly and said, 'If ye looked like that ye wouldn't have to be in a home.' I thought there was some sense in his remark, so I went and did what Lennox had told me to.

Ralph Brereton-Barry played the part of a young bullfighter in the play. He was a very good actor. During his short life he made a name for himself at the Irish Bar, but I think his heart was always in the theatre. I was the world's worst actress. Ralph had once tried to teach me a part but he said I was hopeless, he had never met anyone with less talent for the stage.

Viewing the results of my father's too careful bringing-up of his family, I had decided that if I ever had children I would not interfere in their private lives and would let them have freedom to find their own feet. Paddy and Biddy were a part of a 'gang' of bright young things in Dublin in the 'thirties. So also were David Fitzgerald, who was with us on the night of the burning of Clonard, and his sister Geraldine. Geraldine was one of the few people whom I have known whose childhood dreams came true. From the time she was a very small child she intended to become a film-star, and she did.

As Clonard was a very small house and the bedrooms were on the same floor as the hall and sitting-rooms, the parties which used to arrive after the dances to carry on with bacon and eggs and talk and more fun were rather disturbing. One night I heard cars arriving and the sounds of all the young people enjoying themselves. The sitting-room door was shut but I could hear the piano being played. I was rather surprised, as I knew none of them was a pianist. I thought it might be some foreign station on the radio; the time was about three o'clock in the morning. The player went over a few things in a desultory way and stopped. There was silence—then he began one of the Chopin Ballades. It was magnificent!

As the music came to an end I got up and wrote with a paint-brush on a large sheet of paper, 'Whose is the master hand on the piano?' and left it on the floor outside the sitting-room door. After the applause and the gay voices died down I heard the door open; they were preparing to leave. Then silence again as they found my note and a lot of whispering before they all drove away. In the morning I found the sheet of paper on the floor outside my door. Written on the back of it was, 'Sorry for this nocturnal visit. George Chavchavadze.'

About four o'clock one morning the door of my room opened, the light was turned on and I saw Biddy standing there with her evening dress torn and covered with mud. With a beaming face she said, 'Don't worry, we have had an accident. The car is lying upside down in Phoenix Park. Paddy is hurt, but we got a doctor. He's in bed. David and Geraldine have gone home.' There had been motor-racing in the Park during the week, and after a dance they had evidently gone out there to see what it felt like to be Bira in his Maserati doing 101.6 miles per hour. The old Morris car could not stand the strain, however, and, taking a corner too quickly, just turned upside down.

Biddy seemed to have the whole situation well in hand. I always felt she was a rock of common sense, and it was a comfort to know that she was looking after the rest of them. She was tall and had red-brown hair. She was very popular, and could cook and make her own clothes. She taught me to knit and to drive a car, and there was a lovely relationship between us; she was a mixture of a younger sister and a daughter.

The nineteen-thirties must have been one of the most tragic periods of the whole history of Europe. Two madmen planning the death of millions of their fellow human beings, and there seemed to be nothing much that anyone could do about it.

In Dublin it was a time of memorable parties. There was the Nine Arts Ball with its spectacular floor-shows put on by the School of Art, and private entertaining was as its height. A Swedish consul, Harry Eriksson, and his good-looking wife, Signe, introduced us to the pleasures of delicious Swedish food and drink, which seemed to lead to almost unending and very exciting conversations. I remember a dinner where Oliver Gogarty and Francis Macnamara kept us all entertained, seated at the dinner-table till after midnight. Then there were picnics in the Dublin mountains with schnapps and smorgesbrod, and lunches that went on all the afternoon.

Sometimes a Swedish ship came into the Port of Dublin, and the Captain would give a dinner party and there would be dancing on deck. The parties worked their way West as far as Galway, to the homes of the McDermotts, O'Rorkes and Hemphills. There were wonderful weekends at Tulira Castle, which on the death of Edward Martyn had come into the hands of his nephew, Martin Hemphill. Martin was a very good cook, but his cooking was done with such care and with so much ritual that the dinner never came to the table till late at night, by which time we were all so hungry we would have eaten anything.

It all seemed very gay and hectic. I often wondered what George Moore would have thought of our evenings compared with one he describes in *Ave* when he was staying with 'dear Edward' at Tulira and it was Friday and the salmon had not come from Galway and they sat down to two boiled eggs and a potato each and how indignant George Moore was that he, a Protestant, was compelled to fast and how soon the privations of the meagre meal were forgotten in the wonderful way 'dear Edward' talked of Ibsen and Swift right on into Saturday morning.

André Le Prévost, Commercial Attaché to the French Legation, was living in the Martello Tower at Portmarnock about this time. He gave a party for some Swedish actors and opera singers who had come to Dublin, and after dinner we all went up to the top of the tower where a great bonfire of logs was lit. It blazed up with a roar while the guests piled on more and more logs and sat round singing till it finally died down and the cold night air off the sea drove us back to the large living-room on the first floor where we found that we were all almost black with smoke and smuts.

Francis Macnamara's daughter Caitlin made an appearance in Dublin, a very young and beautiful girl with lovely baby-gold hair. She was even then beginning to show her talent for unconventional behaviour, which she developed still further when she became the wife of Dylan Thomas. Iris Tree was also in Ireland at this time. I remember her at Clonard when Robert and Sylvia Lynd were there too. Iris said that an Irishman's love affair was 'a flash in the pan' and then 'back to the sporting page of the *Evening Herald*'; Sylvia said ruefully, 'Robert never left the sporting page.' Robert laughed his almost silent laugh. I never knew a quieter laugh than Robert Lynd's; his speech was almost as inaudible, which was a pity as he said such good things.

There was a ball one night at the French Embassy and during the evening, in an interval between the dances, a small dark young man went up to the platform where the band was and played Gershwin's *Rhapsody in Blue*, on what I would have called in those days a 'mouth-organ'. It was amazing, an absolute *tour de force*. The performance was applauded and the dancing went on.

A little later in the evening Ralph Brereton-Barry and I were in the hall when we saw the small dark man going out through the hall-door. We went after him. There was a broad flight of steps down to the drive, and there we stopped the young man and said we would like to talk to him. The three of us sat on the steps. I told him how interested I was in his wonderful playing and asked him why he had chosen such a strange instrument. He told us that a 'harmonica' had seemed to him to be the most practical musical instrument to carry about the world, especially for a service man, and that he was giving performances wherever he could get an engagement. His name was Larry Adler.

Ralph used to say the test of a party was: 'Had it one moment of beauty and imagination?' Talking about a party afterwards is half the pleasure.

In spite of the parties, I had begun to spend much more time painting. In 1933 I painted a picture which I liked very much, called 'The Intruder'. It portrayed an imaginary woodland scene with people having a picnic; a female centaur has galloped through the wood and beckons to a young man in the picnic party who is leaping madly forward to follow her. The picture was hung in the Royal Hibernian Academy Exhibition—I had just been made a member of the Academy.

Richard Orpen, who was already an Academician, was very keen that my picture should be bought by the Haverty Trust, which was like the Chantry Bequest in Burlington House. Unfortunately, some of the members of the committee considered that it was 'obscene', so they did not buy it. My meaning, if any, had been that the unknown was more interesting than the known. Next year I sent the picture to the Royal Academy, where it was hung on the line, got good notices, and was caricatured by George Morrow in *Punch* under the title 'The Home Wrecker'.

I painted many of these imaginary scenes and was also getting great pleasure out of painting still-life arrangements with romantic backgrounds of forests and distant figures. I would have liked to have painted still-lifes like some of Gertler's pictures. There was a painting of a china tea-pot in an exhibition of his work that was held in Whitechapel after his death. The profundity and mystery, the beauty of the paint, the queer sense of eternity that it contained! I saw another picture of his in the Redfern Gallery, a Staffordshire man on a horse, that was so final a statement, so completely realized and understood, that it made everything else in the gallery look like tinsel.

One grand thing about painting is that when your picture is finished it *is* finished, it does not have to be cut and glazed, or fired, or cast in bronze.

14

A gastronome's trip across Europe - I perambulate Venice
in an evening dress - Ralph Brereton-Barry recites - Giotto and
Padua overwhelm me - I embark on a second Grand Tour -
Flowers, Erse and Budapest brass-bands - Tête-à-tête with a
lonesome Londoner - Art earns my fare

In August 1932, I left Gordon with the children in Greystones
and I went to Venice with Harry and Signe Eriksson and Ralph
Brereton-Barry. The idea that I should join them on this trip was
arrived at so suddenly that I had no time to get any suitable
clothes. I was so delighted at the thought of seeing Venice that I
was quite content to go with the few things I had.

The Erikssons took their car and we drove there from Calais
by way of the Simplon Pass. I found it all marvellous—the
feeling of coming down from the sun-on-snow air of the Alps
to the perfumed warmth of Italy, and then the lovely Italian
towns and places that John Hughes had talked about in the
modelling-room.

We went to the Certosa of Pavia. I remember Harry Eriksson
saying, 'Give me the money, and with present-day artists and
craftsmen in Sweden I will produce something just as beautiful.'
Harry was a big man with a bald head and horn-rimmed glasses;
he was not good-looking but he had great personal charm. Like
most Swedes he was very interested in food, and he and his wife
Signe knew every restaurant from Calais to Venice.

I remember stopping in some small town and going to some
very special place for dinner. Harry and Signe took some time
choosing what they wanted from the menu. It was terribly hot in
the small room, and when my plate was put in front of me I
took it up, together with my knife and fork, and went outside to
where I had seen some tables and chairs. Harry said indignantly,
'No one eats outside in this restaurant.' I said, 'I do.' A waiter
brought out a cloth and laid a table for me. A few minutes later

Ralph appeared carrying his plate, and after him came Signe carrying hers and laughing at their bad behaviour.

How lovely it was and how happy we were outside in the cool dark night! We looked in through the windows behind us at Harry. He did not know that anyone was looking at him, and was eating carefully and slowly with the intense, absorbed look on his face of someone exploring a mystery.

As children we had been brought up to think that it was almost immoral to enjoy food. If we objected to the eternal mutton-chops which we got for dinner my mother looked surprised and said, 'You have the trees, the birds and the flowers. Food is not important.'

As we continued our journey next day I told Harry how I was almost shocked at the sight of his pleasure in eating. He said, 'A person like you, with luck, may have a few odd moments of ecstasy in your entire life. As for me, if I can get the right food, I can have a moment of ecstasy every twenty-four hours.' All Harry's emotions were as 'outsize' as he was, but he had what he described himself as 'a small hard core of wisdom', which made him a grand person.

In Venice we joined the rest of our party. Martin Hemphill's charming little American wife, and a friend of hers named 'Liz', had been lent a flat in a palace on the Grand Canal. Signe and I shared it with them, while Harry and Ralph and Molly O'Rorke (Master of the Galway Blazers) were in a small hotel somewhere near. They had their meals with us.

Venice was a wonderful experience; especially the first evening, coming suddenly through crowds of people into the Piazza San Marco. The dark velvet-like blue sky glittered with stars, and there was the façade of St Mark's, the campanile, and an orchestra on a platform in the centre of the square just beginning the great majestic chords of the *Meistersinger* overture.

The heat in Venice was appalling, however, for it was August. The other members of the party were experienced travellers, but I was the complete amateur. The other women looked so cool and crisp; I was crumpled and wilting. All the local mosquitoes had congregated round my bed when they heard of my arrival, and no net would keep them out. My face was bitten and swollen beyond recognition, but I did not care. I was in Italy! I was having the time of my life.

During meals in our flat we used to have fierce discussions. Ralph and I protested against the eternal talk on the subject of cooking, for the food was very good and a first-rate cook went with the loan of the flat. Harry quoted Talleyrand as having said, 'Talk about cooking should go with eating.'

I think I must have been giving myself airs about art, and objecting to the other women spending so much time sun-bathing on the Lido. They said I should 'adapt' myself to them. I said they should all 'adapt' themselves to me. I wondered why our conversations should become so animated. Was it the heat? I thought of 'The day is hot, the Capulets abroad, And if we meet we shall not 'scape a brawl.' One evening our dinner ended in a sort of 'rough-house', but no one suffered the fate of Mercutio, and our brawl ended in laughter and friendly feelings.

When the hottest part of the day was over I used to leave them all playing bridge at the Cabina on the Lido and go back to Venice by one of the little motor-boats, to walk about and revel in the beauty of it all. I loved the soft sound of footsteps in the narrow streets, with no other traffic noises. Venice seemed to be full of beautiful young Italian mothers carrying their babies; any of them might have posed as model for a Bellini or Botticelli 'Virgin and Child'.

At about the end of the first week, my scanty wardrobe was all in the laundry and I was reduced to wearing a blue lace evening dress with a long skirt. I had bought a child's large pink linen hat and a pair of white canvas tennis shoes for comfort. I must have looked rather odd, but the rest of the party were quite nice about it—they did not disown me, they were only amused.

There was a party of young English aristocrats and *eleganti* in Venice while we were there. We used to see them sometimes sweeping down the Grand Canal in a large motor-launch, sending the gondolas bumping and swaying about in the wash of their boat. One afternoon at the time that I was reduced to wearing my blue evening dress I was on my way back to Venice from the beach, and to get to the jetty where the motor-boats were moored I had to pass through the large hall of the Excelsior Hotel.

As I entered this place I realized that all the gilded youth were there, laughing and talking at the long bar that ran along one side of the hall. I was rather nervous about my costume, but there was nothing for it but to walk steadily forward on what seemed a very long path to the door at the opposite end, where I could see the sun shining on the motor-boats outside. The talking suddenly died down. I dared not look round, I felt they were all watching me. I hoped I looked like an amiably eccentric lady, who dressed like that because she preferred to do so and not because she had no other clothes.

One evening, after a lot of cooking-talk during dinner, Ralph suddenly began to recite poetry. He did it very well, it was a sort of heritage from his acting days before he became a barrister. To add to the drama of the occasion he addressed his words to me. They were:

I do not love you as I loved
The loves I have loved,
As I may love others:

I know you are not beautiful
As some I loved were beautiful,
As others may be:

I do not hold your counsel dear
As I've held others',
As I still hold some:

And yet
There is no truth but you,
No beauty but you,
No love but you—

And Oh! there is no pain
But you and me.

There was a moment of silence as Ralph finished; everyone was very intrigued. He had spoken with great feeling and intensity and someone asked, 'Who wrote that?' Ralph said, 'I'll give you three guesses.' No one guessed that it was Thomas McGreevy, who in later years became Director of our National Gallery in Dublin. I think Ralph was pleased at the sudden dramatic situation which he had introduced into the cooking conversation.

We went to see the Giottos at Padua, which would have been a great experience for me if I had not upset the whole party by fainting from the heat. I had always thought that I loved the sun till I went to Venice and felt what heat could really be like. The soft sunshine of Ireland was no preparation for the fierce, brassy, almost audible blow that struck you as you stepped out of the shade at Padua. You looked wildly round for another patch of shade to get across the space of sunshine, which seemed as terrible as if it was under a barrage of machine-gun fire. The rest of the party did not seem to mind, except Ralph; I was glad to have a companion in my distress. We felt like two plants that had been brought up in a cool damp grotto.

After my visit to Venice I got such a longing to see new places that I went into Cook & Son's offices in College Green and bought a ticket for a Grand Tour of Central Europe, leaving London on 11 July 1936. Everyone said, 'You are mad—the awful people, the horrible hotels.' They were all wrong. I had the best of hotels, I had paid an extra £3 for that, and the whole trip cost £33 for one month. I liked the people I met on the tour—workers, teachers, nurses, retired elderly people beginning to live; all wanting, like me, to see something of the wonderful Europe we live in.

I think there were about 250 of us. When I went to Liverpool Street Station on the morning of our departure I felt very much alone. A little boy all over buttons with 'Thos. Cook & Son' on his peaked cap came up to me. He was carrying a tray of Malmaison carnations. He held one out to me. I thought he was selling them and shook my head. He said, 'It is a present from Cook & Son.' I was so moved I had to turn away to hide my tears as I fastened the flower into my coat.

We crossed from Harwich to Flushing, and from then on everything was perfect, with no thought of hotel bookings or bothering about luggage or tipping or changing money or paying bills. I had nothing to do but look. We went to Cologne, Dresden, Prague, Budapest, Vienna, Munich and Frankfurt. When our train crossed the frontier into Germany there was a long hold-up at some small station, while uniformed officials came on board to examine our passports. I had an Irish one. The official looked at it and said something to me. I thought he was speaking German and said I did not understand. He repeated what he had said, and I realized he was speaking Irish. I had to confess my ignorance of the language, and asked him how he came to speak it. He said he had taken it as an extra in his university as he thought it might come in useful some time!

I knew very little about what was going on in Europe, but I heard some of my elderly men companions discussing the almost hostile attitude towards us in Munich. I became conscious of a disturbing and sinister feeling everywhere.

The long journey across Hungary to Budapest was somewhat trying. The heat was terrific, and the train was like a furnace. We arrived in Budapest at midnight. To our amazement the train, full of English people, got a staggering reception, flags and cheering and then 'God save the King' played in the station by a desperately loud brass-band while we all stood to attention. I asked my elderly serious-minded fellow-travellers the meaning of this. They said, 'Hungary wants to be friends with Britain in case of war.'

When I arrived at my room in the Hungaria Hotel I went to the window, and there was the milky-grey Danube below me and the lights of Buda and Pest all round, and the night seemed full of music. I could not go to bed. I went down to the street and walked for a long time beside the river. The acacia trees were full of the chirping of cicadas, and every restaurant seemed full of people. Gipsy music and every other kind of music welled out into the night.

On my way back to the hotel, I met another member of our gang. He stopped and said cheerfully, ''Aving a look-see?' I assented. He asked me to have a drink, and we sat outside a café. He began to tell me about his home somewhere outside London, and the golf club which he belonged to and what his handicap was and how his wife and the other ladies took turns about giving tea-parties at the clubhouse, and all the petty jealousy and rivalry there was between the ladies.

My companion went on and on and I listened sympathetically. I felt immersed in the dull, respectable life of some London garden-suburb, while all around us was the strange, hot, still, perfumed night, full of music. When we got up to go, the lights were being turned out in the café. We walked back to the hotel. He thanked me for having listened, and said it had made him feel 'less lonesome'.

Our French Commercial Attaché from Dublin and his wife were in Budapest when I was there and Walter Starkie was staying with them. One evening they took me away from the gang and we dined at a queer little inn in the mountains and drove round many cafés where there were gipsy orchestras; all of them knew Walter as a violinist, and as a writer interested in Tzigane music. They treated him like a king.

Before my Grand Tour, I had left two pictures with Mr Phillips of the Leicester Galleries. He had put them into one of his 'Fame and Promise' shows and had sold them both. I was very pleased to find on my return that my trip had been paid for.

15

*I become a teacher - Testimonial from a model - James
Stephens is commended - Visitors to Katherine Mansfield's
pear tree are turned away - Festivals of talk - Kot
recollects, and polishes his floor - A father speaks up for his
son - Dorothy Brett and the far side of the moon - Curtis
Moffatt attacks an orange and we admire an apple - Gertler
as a raconteur - Picasso alters the life of a night-porter -
Saturday closing prevents a tragedy - I meet Orpen again -
Cream-cakes for a 'Baroness'.*

As the Royal Hibernian Academy premises in Abbey Street had
been destroyed in the 1916 Rising the business of the Academy
was carried on in Richard Orpen's architect's office in South Frederick
Street. Our exhibitions were held in the gallery of the School of
Art. Indeed they still are, as several reasons have prevented us from
building a new gallery and premises.

In 1938 the Academy bought Gogarty's house in Ely Place with
the garden which George Moore writes of in *Salve*, where 'a black-
bird sang all the summer in the biggest apple tree in all Ireland',
and where he and Gogarty walked and talked of poetry. Gogarty,
'the arch-mocker, the author of all the jokes that enable us to live
in Dublin'! Ely Place is different now, it is a parking-place for cars.
The garden is derelict. The Academy had hoped to build a gallery
and an art school there, but the hope is still a dream.

During the years before the Second World War the Academy,
thanks to a small grant from the Government, was still able to run
its free school for drawing and painting. The school was held in
the studio which had once been used by the elder J. B. Yeats, on the
south side of Stephen's Green. As an Academician I took my turn at
teaching. I cannot say I was able to teach the techniques of painting,
but I could give a very good imitation of John Hughes teaching Art.

The class was mostly composed of young girls, and I liked
teaching them very much. I relished the girls' incredulous faces

when I reprimanded them sternly for chattering. It was extraordinary how they could bend apparently intently over their work and keep up an endless flow of chatter to each other, like birds. I would say that it was impossible to draw unless you were in a state of silent, concentrated excitement; they thought this a very strange doctrine.

I would also insist on them using a good, long, well-pointed pencil and a decent bit of paper. They seemed to think any old stump and any crumpled bit of paper would do. I remember telling one girl, who was using a thing like a bit of coal, 'Leonardo himself couldn't draw with that.' She replied haughtily, 'But I *can*.' I believe they enjoyed my teaching, looking on me as a sort of a joke. It was a pleasure to help the students who took their work seriously, though to most of them it was just an amusing way of passing the time.

It was sometimes hard to get models. I remember one girl who had come from London to get away from the bombing. She had been out of work for some time, and was so thin that it was almost painful to look at her; but even in her nearly emaciated state I thought she was beautiful. We engaged her and made an arrangement that she was to have a glass of milk every morning at eleven o'clock. It was pleasant to see her bones disappearing and her appearance returning to normal. When the time came for her to leave us she arrived one morning with a little bunch of flowers which she had bought for me. I was touched and grateful. I had done so little.

There was another model, a dramatic-looking, silent young man, who had also come to Dublin to avoid the war. One day I had been especially fierce to the students, telling them they must use plumb-lines and make measurements, that drawing was not so easy that they could ignore aids; also that they must *know* what they were at, must go close to the model and examine how he was made, note how beautiful and interesting the construction was, and not put pencil to paper without being full of a great love and need to express what they had seen and sought out. I said that no one can draw out of ignorance, that good drawing is the intelligent use of great knowledge.

After the students had gone, I was gathering up my belongings
—I too had been trying to draw the model—when the young man
came out, dressed, from behind the screen where he changed. He
said, 'I was very interested in your teaching. You were so right
about working from a genuine emotion. I looked round at their
blank faces and felt that none of them knew what you were
talking about.'

I was rather surprised, and noticing that he spoke with an
educated English accent, asked him about himself. He said he
wanted to become a writer, and was doing any job he could get
to keep himself alive. He asked me for the drawing I had made and
if I would sign it. I did so and gave it to him. I thought afterwards that perhaps, being poor, he imagined he might be able to
sell it, and was sad for him, as I did not think anyone would want
to buy it. The School finally had to close down, chiefly because of
the expense of fuel, and the problem of procuring it, during the war.

During the nineteen-thirties I kept up my visits to London twice
a year. It was often difficult to get a room, and I stayed in many
different places. I preferred Garland's Hotel to any, in its cul-de-sac
behind the Theatre Royal, Haymarket. I liked the large bust of
the Duke of Wellington, apparently made out of chocolate, on
the first landing, and the indoor garden full of canaries in
cages, all singing like mad.

Kot had made many new friends, among them James Stephens.
Kot had read *The Crock of Gold* when it first came out and had
been a great admirer of Stephens's writing. Now he was as great
an admirer of Stephens as a man, and the feeling was obviously
mutual. I once teased Kot about James, saying, 'He puts on a
leprechaun act for the English people, talking his fantastic talk,
chanting his poems, even making himself look like a leprechaun.'
Kot said, 'Let him be a leprechaun. Behind it is a real man, a real
suffering human being.' Kot always used to say, 'It is good to
suffer', but he could laugh when J. W. N. Sullivan spoke with a
gentle mockery of 'the Higher Suffering'. For Kot, Tolstoy was 'the
greatest and most suffering of human beings.'

Kot would say it was with his body and not with his mind that
he knew what people were like. Some time after Katherine's death

Kot was in his back-garden in Acacia Road. Two women came round the corner of the house, through the side-door. One was elderly and smartly dressed, carrying a little dog. The other was a young negress. Kot took a great dislike to the lady with the dog and ordered them out of his garden, saying it was private property. They said they wanted to see the pear tree that Katherine Mansfield had written about. When they were gone Kot was terribly sorry, because of the black girl; he wished he had been kind to them since she had come to see Katherine's pear tree.

Sometimes we wondered how Kot lived, for no one ever saw him working. We knew he had done translations of Russian books and that during the First War, between the May and October Russian Revolutions in 1917, he had been a correspondent for a paper called the *Bourse Gazette*. He taught Russian to Gyp Wells and his father before they went to London in 1920. At one time he was a reader for a London publisher, and helped many young writers. Indeed, he helped many people in different ways, but he was very secretive about it.

Conversation is one of the greatest pleasures and Kot was wonderful to talk to; he seemed to know what you were trying to say almost before you could formulate the words yourself. We sometimes used to laugh at the festivals of talk that we indulged in. Once we had gone on for hours about Shakespeare (I had just seen Gielgud as Lear) when I got up to go : it was getting late. I heard myself say solemnly, 'Good night, sweet prince; and flights of angels sing thee to thy rest.' Kot began to laugh at being called 'sweet prince'; I always felt pleased if I made Kot laugh. I think it was Shaw who said, 'The Irish are a people who have an insane desire to make each other laugh.' But laughter is one of the lovely things of life, and worth remembering.

For Kot people were either 'ordinary' or 'exceptional', and these two kinds were miles apart. I remember some people coming to tea in his kitchen who were not 'exceptional'. We made pleasant conversation. When Kot showed them out, he came back in a state of exhaustion. He leaned on the table, white in the face, and said, 'Oh, the ordinariness of ordinary people!'

When talking about his childhood, he told me of his earliest memory. It was of a night when a man had been drowned. The people of his village had no knowledge of present-day methods of artificial respiration. The drowned man was put on a horse, in front of the rider, then the horse was galloped as hard as possible; apparently breathing was sometimes restored by this process.

Kot stood, a very small child with his family, in the badly lit village street. It was night. He watched the people tie the drowned man to the rider on the horse, then they galloped away into the distance. All waited till the sounds of the galloping hooves approached the village from the other end, the rider having gone round in a wide circle. Kot could see the gleaming white face of the drowned man bobbing about and hear the wails of the people as the horse thundered past, going round and round the village. Each time it returned there was the white face and the wailing.

Another time he told me how his father used to chant some plain-song or psalm every Saturday night while the children all sat round waiting for the stars to come out. The appearance of the stars ended the Sabbath and marked the beginning of the ordinary week. As Kot was telling me this he took a piece of paper out of a drawer, on which a few bars of music had been written by some musical friend. He asked me if I could sing it. I could not manage the Hebrew words but I sang the notes. I said, 'Sing it with me.' We sang it together over and over again. It was getting dusk, and we kept on singing and looking out of the window at the sky over Acacia Road, waiting for the stars to appear. Kot had a strange, hypnotized look on his face as if he was back again in his childhood. The street-lamps lit up, but no stars. We turned again to the Russian tea.

People writing books about Katherine used to go to Kot to get information about her or just to talk about her. Some of them he dismissed at once, others he tried to help. He never approved of any book written about Katherine, it was always the work of some 'inferior mind'. I spoke of one of these books, which I thought had some truth in it about her, praising it. He said, 'The only one true statement in it was that she was born in New Zealand.'

Katherine told me that there had once been a 'Sonia' in Kot's life. They had been fellow-students of Kiev University. Kot had said,

Mark Gertler, 1923

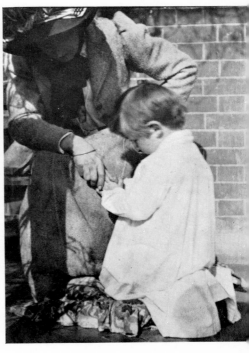

Samuel Beckett at his mother's knee

On the afternoon of the first daylight air-raid on London, July 17, 1917. The author (with parasol), Humbert Wolfe, Amber Blanco White: Malcolm (seated on the ground with Biddy), Marjorie, Paddy

Katherine Mansfield,
9 Selwood Terrace, London, 1914

S. S. Koteliansky, James
Stephens, Lady Ottoline
Morrell, 10 Gower Street,
London, 1935

'Wherever Sonia was there was laughter and happiness.' The attachment lasted for three years, then another man took Kot's place. According to Katherine, 'One day Kot went to her house as usual, rolling his Russian cigarettes. She just shut the door in his face.' He liked her for ending it that way: no excuses, no apologies, no explanations. Sonia and her new friend were later arrested as revolutionaries and sent to Siberia. Kot never heard what became of them.

In London I spent the mornings going to picture exhibitions or walking for miles just to enjoy the London streets and shop-windows. Every afternoon I sat at Kot's kitchen table.

Kot used to say that a man's house is himself. His house was scrubbed and polished and dusted, with a special place for every cup, plate, book or piece of paper. He was an expert launderer and did all his own washing, even the blankets. He was also a good cook and enjoyed cooking little suppers for his friends. He once showed me how a Russian servant polished the floor; he had dusters tied round his feet, and slid about on his hall-floor swishing from side to side in a sort of wild dance.

The polish on his hall-floor was really dangerous. There were a couple of small rugs and it was almost fatal to step on one of them, they just flew from under your feet and you sat down with a bang. When Kot opened his hall-door he had to warn the visitor to be careful; he clung on to you and you clung on to him till you could get a grip of the banisters and work your way into the sitting-room. The danger of breaking your bones was so great that I gave up going to the hall-door. On entering the little bit of front-garden you could see Kot sitting at his kitchen table through the half-basement window, then you made a sign that you were going round by the side-door which led into the scullery. There he would meet you and say, 'It is good that you have come', and lead the way into the kitchen where so much Russian tea was drunk and where the conversation went on almost as if there had not been any break since the last time.

Once a week Kot and his friends dined in a restaurant in the Tottenham Court Road. He and Gertler called this place 'The Wr-r-rotten Jews'. One evening I went there to meet them. There sat W. J. Turner, J. W. N. Sullivan, Kot and Gertler. Before James arrived Kot said that we must be careful not to mention James's son, who was a bit wild and had got into trouble, all of which had been reported in the newspapers that morning. When Stephens came he must have been aware of the constraint. Sullivan was talking of some book that he had read which stated that the only enemy the human race really had was the 'Germ'. James Stephens spoke. He said, 'I have a son (everyone's attention was riveted on him in horrified silence). I'll back my son against any germ—anywhere.' There was rather embarrassed laughter, and the constraint was broken. We all loved James.

Gertler's laughter was a glorious thing. It seemed to bend him and shake him till all the curly hair above his forehead was jumping and bobbing about. He could laugh at such silly things that it was a great pleasure to be with him. Dorothy Brett, Gertler and I were once walking along Acacia Road from Kot's house. On our left a full moon was rising over the trees and houses, the face on the moon very clearly marked. Brett gazed up at it and said sentimentally, 'I wonder what is on the other side of the moon?' I said, 'Hair!' I had to speak rather loudly as Brett was somewhat deaf. Gertler began to laugh; Brett looked bewildered and turned to me asking, 'What did you say?' Again I shouted, 'Hair!' Gertler and I were both laughing wildly, Gertler with his curls shaking and bobbing.

On one of my visits to London I stayed at the Tour Eiffel in Charlotte Street. Gertler and I had been to a cinema and were having some supper. At the same table were sitting Iris Tree and her first husband, Curtis Moffatt. There was also an elegant young man whom I did not know. Otherwise the place was empty. Stulick, the proprietor, was asleep with his head resting in his arms at another table; Iris and the elegant young man were talking quietly about people they had known; Curtis Moffatt was eating oranges in a horrible way, tearing them open and biting into the centre of them with his teeth.

Iris said that she had lately been in Paris and met Charlie Chaplin, and that it was sad to see that his hair was growing grey. Curtis Moffatt suddenly looked up, his face dripping with orange-juice, and said abruptly, 'The hair on the head does not matter. It is when the pubic hair turns grey!' He dived back into his orange. I laughed and Gertler began to laugh, and went on laughing and bending and tossing his head and saying through his laughter, 'You must excuse my friend. She is from Ireland, she is not used to such conversation.'

I remember another night in L'Étoile, when Gertler and I had finished dinner and were just leaving the restaurant, and both stopped to look at an apple on a table. It was mysterious and beautiful. It had two shadows thrown from two different lights which partly overlapped each other. We stood there gazing. The little Italian wife of the proprietor came up to us and said in her pretty foreign English, 'You may eat eet if you like.' It was difficult to explain that we only wanted to look at it.

Gertler had a great talent for telling stories about himself in which he appeared in a ludicrous light. He was once staying at the house of some rich people where he had a bathroom off his bedroom, but he could not find out how to get the water into the bath. He was so afraid that the maids might think that he had not taken a bath that he damped the bath-towel under the tap in the basin.

I remember Gertler saying rather bitterly about his girl-friends, 'All women are looking for a knight in armour, on a white horse, beside a lake, at sunset.' I think he hated anything so romantic and vague. He used to make funny stories out of his most tragic moments. The first time he tried to take his life was when he developed tuberculosis and had to go to a sanatorium in Scotland. He cut the veins in his wrists but he was bandaged up and put to bed before much harm was done. That night he was not to be left alone, and the only person who could be found to stay with him was the night-porter. On the table of Gertler's room was a large book of reproductions of Picasso drawings and paintings, and to pass the long hours the porter looked through this book. Gertler pretended to be asleep. He watched the man slowly turning the pages, then turning the book upside down and from side to side. When he came to the end he went back to the beginning again and so the night passed. Gertler said afterwards, 'That night-porter was never the same man again.'

At dinner one night Gertler and I were talking together of growing older. He said his one fear had been that he might feel less acutely about everything, but to his great delight he found that he felt everything even more intensely. He talked of painting, and said that every emotion that he felt in ordinary life was amplified a hundredfold in painting—every anguish, every ecstasy, every sort of pain and suffering, every kind of joy and contentment.

We talked of love and falling in love. He said that, for him, ten years was about the length of time that being in love could last. He said that it was ten years to the day from the time he had fallen in love with Carrington in the Slade to the time when he heard that she was going to marry someone else. He was so shattered that he felt that nothing but a revolver could end his pain. He went out to buy one, but found it was Saturday afternoon and all the shops were shut. He could laugh at his sufferings and we both agreed that we liked the Chaucer poem 'Merciless Beaute' with its charming refrain:

> Sin I fro Love escaped am so fat
> I never think to ben in his prison lene;
> Sin I am free, I count him not a bene.

We talked about Orpen and the enormous financial success he had had with his painting. At one time an enterprising American syndicate had offered him a million dollars to go to America and paint thirty portraits. He refused; he had as many orders for portraits from £2,000 to £3,000 as he could cope with in London. I had just been to the Imperial War Museum in Lambeth to have another look at Orpen's 1914-18 War pictures which he had presented to the nation. I was very impressed by his beauty-sense, the lovely paint and the joy of painting. Oliver Gogarty said after Orpen's death, 'He never got under the surface till he got under the ground', but even the surface of things can be beautiful, mysterious and worth recording. The quality that makes a really great work of art, that sense of the supernatural, is something that comes like a thief in the night without the artist's knowledge or intent.

I told Gertler how Orpen and I had gone on writing amusing

illustrated letters to each other all through the war and afterwards. Finally the letters got fewer and farther between and
came to an end. I had only seen Orpen a few times after I was
married. After the death of his parents he gave up going to Ireland.
Gertler said, 'Why don't you ring him up and meet him again?'
(At this time I was on one of my visits to London.) I rang Orpen,
and he suggested we should meet at the Berkeley the following day.

I went, but I knew at once that it was all wrong. He was a
completely different person, perhaps I was too. The tension, the
strain was terrible! I could not have believed that such a situation
would have been possible between us. We tried to talk about long-
ago summer days and bathing at Howth or Portmarnock beach.
It was impossible. He had quarrelled with Gogarty and 'the Boss'.
I tried to tell him about my new friends. He was not interested.
I cut our meeting as short as possible, to his evident relief.

The last time I saw Frieda was some years after Lawrence's death
in 1930. She was staying in London with a Russian Revolutionary
woman-friend whom Kot was anxious to meet, and we went to
tea with them at their hotel. Frieda's hair was cut short, she had
grown very fat and wore a cloak. She looked like a jolly friar. Kot
and the Russian woman talked Russian to each other. Frieda and I
gossiped happily about old times.

She was eating large cream-cakes with great relish, cream was
all round her mouth and over her cheeks. After a while Kot seemed
to have taken a dislike to the Russian woman. They were silent and
he was regarding Frieda with a look of loathing. She was very
conscious of this and began defending herself with, 'Lawrence
wanted me to be happy, Lawrence always wanted me to be happy',
almost on the verge of tears.

16

*Kot as 'The Lion of Judah' - I learn of Gertler's death - The
shadows of war deepen - Conflict watched from a neutral
land - Biddy plays her part - I visit old haunts under fire -
Servants artistic, pregnant and insane - Life in a kitchen-sink -
Simon heads for home - Death of my daughter*

In 1938 James Stephens published a little book of verse titled *Kings
and the Moon;* in it there is a poem called 'The Lion of Judah' about
Kot. It is rather long to quote in full, it is also rather obscure. In
fact, the only bit I can understand is the first verse:

> Tell now what is happening
> On the sole Arabian tree
> There is no song in anything
> No tale of glee.

This poem was written just before the Second World War, when
Kot was beginning to despair of the human race. Gertler's tragic
death in 1939 was another source of great unhappiness for him.
I remember Kot saying, 'Gertler, who loved life, how could he have
killed himself?'

Though Gertler recovered from tuberculosis, his health was
not robust, so he never had to do military service. In the spring
of 1930 he married Marjorie Hodgkinson, who had also been
at the Slade. They had one little boy who was very delicate as a
baby, and Gertler suffered tortures of anxiety over him and Marjorie. When he told me of the baby's arrival he said, 'It was awful!
Marjorie nearly died, the baby nearly died, and I nearly died.'

In the summer of 1939 he had a show of pictures at the Lefevre
Gallery which was not a success. He was terribly depressed by the
criticism he received in the papers, also by the horrors of Hitler's
anti-Jewish campaign. His financial position and family matters
began to make life unbearable for him. It was Kot who wrote to

tell me of Gertler's death. He was to have gone to tea with Kot
—he did not appear. Kot began to get anxious, for he knew Gertler
had been suffering great depression, and went to his studio. 'He
was lying as if asleep on a mattress beside the gas-fire.'

Gertler was still young. In spite of his ill-health (he had been
forced to spend some time in a sanatorium) he managed to get
through an immense amount of work, was a constant exhibitor
at the New English Art Club and the London Group, and had many
one-man shows at the Leicester Galleries, the Lefevre Gallery and
Agnew's. The style of his painting had developed and changed,
and the sincerity of his work was deeply impressive; it seems strange
that so good a painter should have had so little recognition since
his death.

I was in London during Chamberlain's visits to Hitler, when no
one seemed to know what to do or how to do it. The prevailing
mood was one of awful uncertainty, with half-hearted preparations, such as dug-out shelters being made in the parks, and
everyone still almost wildly hoping that a miracle would happen
and that there would not be a war—that we should all wake
up and find that Hitler had only been a bad dream. Kot's black-
ness was profound. Then came the day when Hitler went too
far.

I was again in London when the Chamberlain Government was
dissolved. Kot and I listened to the Churchill broadcast, 'the blood
and sweat and tears' speech. It was terrifying and moving. Kot said
when it was over, 'The mantle of a Leader has fallen on him. In
his hands lies the historical destiny of the British people.' He had
an enormous admiration and affection for Churchill. Kot remained
in Acacia Road during the war. His hate of Hitler would not let
him be driven away, though even Stephens went to live in the
country.

As Ireland had decided to remain neutral, most of the war news
was censored in the newspapers. We had to depend very much on
the B.B.C. to know what was going on. Some tentative preparations
were made to combat a possible invasion by the Germans; but we
knew that if Hitler wanted to invade Ireland there was nothing that
we could do to stop him.

Some people in Dublin even admired Hitler, and there was a certain amount of pro-German feeling. I remember passing a group of working men in the street and hearing one of them say proudly, 'Ye know, Hitler has a very high opinion of the Irish people.' Apparently he spoke with knowledge and authority. The other workmen looked at him with admiration.

Because of our neutrality Dublin by night was brightly illuminated, but in spite of these lights a few bombs and a land-mine were dropped on the city. It was about four o'clock in the morning. We heard the roar of a bomber flying low, then the crash of exploding bombs getting nearer. The last one fell in a field at the bottom of our garden. We heard the shower of stones and earth falling on the roof of the house.

In 1940 we left Clonard and moved into an old Georgian house farther away from Dublin. It had a river running through the grounds and an old ruined mill. I was sorry to leave the other house, but the fields round it had been built over and it was an entirely different place from what it had been when we went there. The new house needed a lot of doing up, but it was very interesting making it habitable and planning a garden. We made a swimming-pool in the river, and laid out a tennis-court. As Michael was at school quite near us and later at Trinity College, the place was always full of young people. For the first few years of the war it was almost impossible to get out of Ireland. There were no permits for unofficial travelling.

Biddy had just finished a brilliant career at Trinity and graduated with a first-class moderatorship in Experimental Science. She seemed to have a natural flair for mathematics which was probably a heritage from a relative on her Grandmother Campbell's side of the family. This grandmother had been a Miss McCullagh who had a great-uncle, James McCullagh, a very distinguished mathematician. There is a bust of him by a sculptor named Christopher Moore in the Long Room of Trinity College Library. Biddy had also distinguished herself in the world of sport: she had been a successful yachting helmsman, a member of the Irish International Lacrosse Team and a winner of the Squash Racquets Championship. She managed to get herself a post as a research chemist in the Ministry of Aircraft Production in London, and while she was there I was allowed a permit to visit her.

On my trips to London I also saw Kot. We walked round looking at the terrible devastation in St. John's Wood, while he told me of terrible nights of bombs and burnings. There was a dairy on his road where a lot of valuable van-horses were stabled. One night the dairy was burning, there were fires all round, everything seemed aflame. Kot told me how he watched the van-drivers leading out the frightened animals, speaking comfortingly to them, patting them, soothing them—he was greatly impressed by the men being so calm and unperturbed. He found the terrible dust from the bombings very hard to cope with, the *cœur de lion* dust as he called it. It was all over his spotless house, his food and everything.

It was good to see Biddy so happy and keen about her work. She had a flat in Petty France, near Victoria Street, where there were other Irish friends of hers also working in M.A.P. They all seemed to be as cheerful, calm and unperturbed as the stablemen in Kot's dairy.

Because of our neutrality Kot said, 'The Irish are fleas and lice.' I tried to tell him of the large percentage of Irishmen in the Forces and how my son Michael's Irish public school boasted of nine Generals serving, and how most of the English Generals were Irish. Kot was amused and proud of James Stephens, who because of our neutrality had put a notice in *The Times* saying that for the duration of the war he wished to be considered an Englishman.

The 'blitz' was over, the Battle of Britain had been fought and won, there were still occasional air-raids, although the flying-bombs had not yet started. On my short visits to London what was most terrifying to me was the black-out on nights when there was not a trace of a moon—the taxis creeping along with one tiny glimmer of a head-light, people bumping into each other or falling over something, insane laughter coming out of the darkness and the awful feeling of not knowing where you were or which way you were going.

One lovely morning I wandered through the ruined streets and warehouses round St Mary-le-Bow. I was sitting on a bit of broken wall, in the sunshine, when a taxi drove up and stopped near me and several American soldiers got out. They had the freshly laundered and ironed look that all G.I.s have, and were rather a contrast to the blackened ruins round us. They asked the taxi-driver to wait for them; they too wanted to walk about and look at the destruction. The taxi-driver lit his pipe and settled down to wait. I also waited. I was curious to know what the Americans would feel about it all. After about twenty minutes they returned, and the taxi-driver said cheerfully and proudly, 'Well, did you like it?' The Americans got into the taxi in silence and drove away. I was left wondering whether they had liked it or not.

As far as the housekeeping was concerned, 1940 was a very awkward time for us to have moved farther away from shops which had very little petrol for delivering goods. There were few buses and there was no petrol for private motoring. Our two perfect maids found life too difficult and lonely and soon left us. After that it was almost impossible to get anyone. We were so far from Dublin, and the buses were so few and far between, that the only maids who would come to us were people whom no one else would employ.

We had what Thurber calls 'A Sequence of Servants'. One of them was an artist. I think she never knew what an artist was till she came to me and saw my paintings, then she became so interested that she started making drawings herself. I thought she had talent and bought her a water-colour paint-box and drawing-book, and thereafter she spent most of her time in her bedroom, painting. When she started to paint *on* my pictures, I thought it was time for her to go. After her departure I found the paint-box and drawing materials shoved into an old stove in the boiler-room; she had given up Art.

Another girl we employed was going to have a baby. When I found this out I was all ready to give help and comfort, but she seemed delighted with herself, and said, 'He will have to give me twelve shillings and sixpence a week and I will get ten pounds maternity benefit when the child is born.' It was as if she had gone in for Big Business.

Another poor creature was not right in her head and locked herself into her room, saying she was going to commit suicide. I had to climb through the window and remove the bottle of disinfectant that she intended to drink. It was a great relief to get her comfortably into a mental home.

I had made a sitting-room for the maids out of a room which had a kitchen-sink in one corner, and had put a curtain round the sink as it would no longer be in use. One day I went into this room and, thinking something about the curtain looked rather suspicious, pulled it aside to find a completely unknown girl sitting on the draining-board with her feet in the sink. There were tears and explanations, and the cook came running from the kitchen. The strange girl was her sister, out of a job, who had been living in the sink for some days.

There were many other maids, good, bad and appalling. As the years went on the bus service improved and we were able to obtain the 'treasures' which we have today; but in those days I often thought of Clonard with longing.

One day I was in the garden talking to Cook, our gardener. He was finding the making of an entirely new garden in an exposed plot rather a heart-breaking job. He had loved the little sheltered place at Clonard and the gate lodge where he had been so happy when newly married and where his child had been born. I spoke of how much I had liked our little house there, so covered with creepers that at night with the windows open one could hear the birds rustling the leaves as they were roosting, or shuffling about round their nests and whispering together. Cook spoke with a homesick affection for every square yard of the garden he had tended for almost twenty years. I spoke of the happy evenings when Ralph used to come out from the Law Courts and he and I would play croquet, and of the pond in the back field with the flat-bottomed boats that Tom Casement had made for the children. In spite of the larger beauties of our new home, Clonard seemed a lost Eden.

While we talked Biddy's cocker spaniel dog Simon was beside us, just scratching himself or sniffing about, not apparently taking any notice of our talk. We came to the end of what we had to say; Cook went on with his work and I went into the house. That evening Simon was not to be found anywhere. I did not worry as

171

he and the other dog often went wandering. But the other dog was still here. Three days passed and still no Simon. I was putting up notices in the Post Office, making inquiries all around and getting very upset, when on the fourth morning the phone rang and a woman's voice said, 'I am ringing up from Clonard, Kimmage Road. A dog arrived here yesterday in a very exhausted condition. We have just discovered your name and this address on his collar.' I rang at once for a taxi to come and take me to him.

It was strange to walk into my own house and find other people and other furniture in it. We sat in a little room where I used to paint, with a door on to a balcony and steps down into the garden. They told me how they had been sitting in this room the evening before when a very tired dog came climbing up the steps and, ignoring everyone, lay down on the hearth-rug and with a great sigh fell asleep. When he woke they gave him milk and a biscuit but he only seemed anxious to explore the house. He went into every room and then down to the lodge, where he had remained. Someone went to get him and I waited. When Simon saw me his excitement was overwhelming; he cried out loud and I wept.

During the years in which we lived in Clonard, Ralph Brereton-Barry had been closely associated with our life there, and his gay and amusing presence seemed still to exist in the room where we sat. My very emotional state on my reunion with Simon was largely due to the fact that at that time Ralph was lying dangerously ill in a fever hospital with typhoid, which he had contracted in some country town where he had gone on circuit—he did not recover.

The lady of the house was very kind and comforted us. Then I proceeded to take my leave. Simon came as far as the hall-door. I went on ahead calling him to follow me, but he would not move. He stood on the steps barking in a sort of despairing way as if he was trying to say, 'I have found our home after three days and nights of travelling on roads which I have never been on before except in a motor-car, I have suffered and struggled on in my effort to find this place, and now you want us to leave it again.'

I could not explain the situation to him, but I remembered how much he enjoyed driving in a car and said, 'Come for a drive, Simon.' Very doubtfully and suspiciously he came after me. When we had started he seemed quite happy and once back at Rockbrook he never again had any inclination to leave it. Biddy loved her two dogs, and in my next letter to her I told her the story of Simon's return to Clonard, and of how he had evidently become conscious of Cook's and my feelings about the place and something in him had driven him to find it again.

In 1943 Biddy had married a colleague in her Department. In 1944 they were both killed by a flying-bomb one night in their little house in a mews off Prince's Gate, South Kensington. Her last letters had been full of excitement about the opening of the Second Front. She was happy in her marriage and looking forward to the end of the war.

17

*Governor into gardener - Rubble in peacetime sunlight - Kot
in grim mood - Dr Fulton admits to a defect of character - I
talk of music and quote Browning - Family reunions - A wasp
interrupts Feliks Topolski - Sam Beckett helps an invalid - A
businessman turns humorist - The Dáil is not amused - Nor
is Jack Yeats - Another author in the family - Literary dis-
courses over Russian tea - Cynthia Stephens victrix - Dublin
espouses contemporary art - I take wing - An unbeliever's
creed*

I find it difficult to make myself remember those later years of the
Second World War. In an effort to try to do something to help
I kept on endlessly knitting comforts for the troops, though for a
while it was even questionable as to whether Irish neutrality could
permit such a thing. I cannot even remember the war ending or
whether there was any rejoicing. Life just went on.

It was about this time that Gordon, who was already Director
of many different companies became Governor of the Bank of
Ireland. The world of finance into which he had fallen exercised a
strong fascination for him. But it never took him in—although he
became one of the most distinguished figures in Irish Banking. He
would have preferred to have been a writer of plays, a noise in
the theatre rather than a power in the city.

As well as all his Company Director activities he was now deeply
involved in getting rid of some of the brambles, bracken and gorse
on our new land. There were trees to be planted, a garden to be
planned, and old farmhouse buildings to be repaired; he was also
laying the foundations in roses and rhododendrons of the lovely
place which Rockbrook is today.

After 1944 I did not go to London again till the war was over.
It was good, when at last I went, to find Kot still sitting at his
kitchen table and his friends still coming to visit him. He had been

shocked that the Irish Government was so bound by its neutrality formalities and its diplomatic usage that de Valera sent his 'condolences' to the German Embassy when Hitler's death was announced.

I went to look at Garland's Hotel. It had had a direct hit. As I was standing on the pavement wondering what had become of all the friendly people who had worked there, a young, cheerful voice addressed me: 'Have you come back to see what has happened to us?' A girl was polishing the brasses on a hall-door beside me, and I recognized her as one of the girls from the reception desk. She seemed the very spirit of the city; polishing the knocker, carrying on smiling and unconquered. We surveyed the ruins of the hotel at the end of the cul-de-sac and she told me about the night the bomb fell and who had survived and how lucky it was that the hotel had been almost empty at the time; most of the staff had retired to their own premises in the house where she was now.

I went to Prince's Gate Mews. The rubble had all been cleared away from the place where Biddy's and Robbie's house had stood. In the dust I could make out the foundations of the small row of houses, and I found the place where their hall-door had been and part of the tiled floor of the hall. The sun was shining, the sky was blue. In the other part of the mews there were chauffeurs cleaning cars and whistling or shouting gaily to each other. The voices of the men, the life that was going on, seemed to have no reality.

Though Hitler had gone there were still the Bolshevists and Stalin to cast a black shadow over Kot. Because of them his talk was full of hate; people were all 'horrors and blighters'. One Thursday tea-time he was talking about a man that he had seen eating in a restaurant: 'It was such a horrible sight.' All men had become loathsome and hideous because of the way this man was eating and *enjoying* his food.

I told him how, that morning on my way to Acacia Road, I had gone into a place in Oxford Street to get some lunch. It was a dreary and horrible restaurant, full of dull and ugly people and tired waitresses. Suddenly a little child broke away from its mother and came running between the tables, laughing and giving piercing cries of delight. It was as if a miracle had happened. The place seemed to light up. There were smiles on every face. People were trying to entice the child to their tables. Everyone became friendly with everyone else; the tired waitresses suddenly had wings to their feet. I said, 'If your man had been there, he too would have become beautiful and friendly.' Kot said, 'If my man had been there he would have eaten that child.' We all laughed, which pleased him, though he continued in his grim mood.

I think Dr Fulton was there that afternoon. He was keeper in the Department of Oriental Printed Books and Manuscripts at the British Museum and Kot had a great affection for him. He alluded to him as 'little Fulton', more as a term of endearment than as a description of his size. I remember Kot taking down another cup and saucer from the dresser in expectation of Dr Fulton's arrival, and saying sadly 'Little Fulton, he ruins his nice tea by putting milk in it.'

One afternoon Dr Fulton spoke to me about Paddy's golf. I think he had been following Paddy in some championship matches in the newspapers. He went on to speak of other games and admitted shyly that as a young man he had played Rugby for England. Kot listened with interest but said nothing. I could not help feeling that Dr Fulton's statement was for Kot almost a revelation of a defect in his friend. I sometimes spoke to Kot about Gordon's great interest in sport and his talent for anything to do with a ball game; also of his amazing knowledge of every horse which had ever won a race or been an 'also ran'. To Gordon the world of sport and games was as full of magic and mystery as the world of art to the painter. To Kot this attribute was inexplicable, something almost adolescent of which he could not help feeling slightly contemptuous.

Kot had often spoken with pride and affection of a friend of his named Violet Schiff. He had told me how she and her husband, a writer who used the pen-name of Stephen Hudson, had been friends of Proust and Oscar Wilde and how her sister, Ada Leverson, had befriended Wilde when nearly everyone else was against him. He took me to her house in Ilchester Place to meet her.

Kot had never mentioned music in connection with Violet Schiff, but one had only to enter her room to know how important it was in her life. There stood the grand piano with no vestige of any object on its broad black surface and the keyboard open. We talked of music and she put a record on the radiogram, a lovely warm contralto singing some little German folk-song. I asked whose voice it was, she said it was herself. As a sort of experiment she had had some records made, and had tried singing an octave lower than she had done as a younger woman. The records were quite lovely—French and Italian songs, some to her own accompaniment. As Kot and I left the house I scolded him for not having told me that she was a musician, although he had spoken of her work as a translator. I felt that his attitude towards her music was rather like what he felt about Dr Fulton's football.

Music meant little to Kot, though he did lay claim to having a definite feeling for Beethoven. He knew a lot about composers and musicians and the theory of music in general. He had known Artur Schnabel and they had evidently liked each other. Kot said, 'He is not like a musician; he is a very intelligent man.' At this I became indignant at the implied insult to musicians, and quoted Browning:

Sorrow is hard to bear, and doubt is slow to clear,
 Each sufferer says his say, his scheme of the weal and woe:
But God has a few of us whom he whispers in the ear;
 The rest may reason and welcome: 'tis we musicians know.

Kot did not know the poem. We looked it up in a copy of Browning that Lady Ottoline had given him—the last line was underlined.

When it was possible to move about the world again, Marjorie came from New Zealand with her lovely daughter, and later her sons came too. Dorothy also came from South Africa with her fine grown-up family. We had a very pleasant feeling that we shared in the parentage of the children. I heard Marjorie talking of Paddy as if she were his mother, and said, 'But Paddy is *my* son.' Marjorie corrected me: '*Our* son.'

In the years after the Second World War our house still retained its 'caravanserai' character; friends came and brought their friends and Sunday evening was still a time of meeting. Sooner or later everyone who is anyone seems to visit Ireland, and many of these visitors have found their way to Rockbrook.

I remember Thornton Wilder talking so well about the 'Golden Girls of Literature', with Natasha Rostov as the most golden of the lot. Another night Feliks Topolski was talking of journalism in painting from Giotto to the present day, when one member of the party who had just left the room returned saying, 'The most wonderful thing you ever saw is happening in the bathroom.' We all rose up like a flock of birds and swept upstairs to crowd into the little room.

On the small rod which held the window curtains a queen wasp was starting to build her nest. It was like a tiny inverted cup. The wasp was going slowly round spreading some grey filmy stuff on the edges. We were all so in sympathy with the wasp that we decided to keep the door shut so that she should not be disturbed. I remember that Marjorie was staying with us at that time, and next morning she and I, full of curiosity, went to see how the wasp was getting on. The nest was now as big as a tea-cup, upside down, but there was no sign of the wasp. I said, 'Perhaps she is inside hanging up her pictures.' Marjorie listened for a second and said, 'I can't hear any hammering.' The wasp had evidently decided that the bathroom was not a suitable place. It was just as well, I was not very keen to have a wasp's nest in the house.

After 'the Boss' died, his wife Cissie slowly became crippled with arthritis. I used to go to see her in her house by the sea at Raheny where she lived with some of her family. She often spoke of her nephew Sam Beckett with great affection, and when he came from Paris to see his mother at Foxrock he went to visit Cissie also. He would take her for a drive or a turn in her wheel-chair along the sea-road. She used to say with pleasure, 'Sam was here' or 'Sam is coming'.

When I read *End Game* I recognized Cissie in Hamm. The play was full of allusions to things in her life, even the old telescope which Tom Casement had given me and I had passed on to her to amuse herself with by watching ships in Dublin Bay or seabirds feeding on the sands when the tide was out. She used to make jokes about her tragic condition. She once asked me to 'straighten up the statue'—she was leaning sideways in her chair and her arthritis had made her body heavy and hard and stiff like marble. As I did what she asked I saw tears of laughter in her eyes. Cissie finished her days in a rather dreary home for old people. I gathered from her that Sam still came to see her and that his visits brought her much happiness.

As time went on I had an added interest in going to London. Paddy was now married and living near Maidenhead with his wife and little daughter. He had been to school at Rossall, in Lancashire, and had spent four terms at Oxford not really knowing what he wanted to do. I had always felt that he had a talent for comic writing, his letters from school were so funny that I used to send them on to Marjorie and Dorothy as I knew they would be as much amused as I was. Gordon had had important connections with the Siemens-Schuckert Company when they were working on the Shannon scheme to give electricity to Ireland. As Paddy had expressed a wish to learn a foreign language and see Europe, Gordon got him a position with this firm in Munich. This was about 1937.

During the Second World War a large double-page aerial photograph appeared in some English weekly paper of the devastation done by British bombers to the Siemens-Schuckert works. I showed it to Paddy and asked him to point out to me where his office was. He said he never knew where it was; though he had been there for three years, he could never find the same place twice. The offices all looked the same, so he just went into any place where he saw a vacant stool at a desk and sat there. This statement could not have been quite correct, as the firm had written to Gordon expressing their approval of Paddy's work and saying they would like to send him to South America on some project, but Paddy did not want to be a businessman.

He went to Paris for a while and returned to Dublin to work on the *Irish Times* as second leader-writer, reporter, book-page editor, film-critic and Parliamentary correspondent; he also wrote a daily column under the title 'An Irishman's Diary' which kept Dublin laughing for years. His account of the proceedings in the Irish Parliament (the Dáil) was such hilarious nonsense that the members

179

began to protest. Among the flippancies he wrote about the Dáil was one on 'the effect of the lady members' spring-suiting on the Farmers' Party'.

When the Second World War broke out Paddy joined the newly formed Irish Marine Service and spent four years searching in-coming ships in Dublin Bay. We never quite knew what he was searching for. In 1946 he was offered a job on an English paper, went to London and has remained there ever since. He has pub-lished many very funny books, some of them superbly illustrated by Ronald Searle. In more recent years he has had a weekly column in the *Sunday Times* which has added to his reputation for comedy with, at times, an added quality of something almost amounting to wisdom.

Jack Yeats once said that there was no such thing as comic writing, and to try to prove that he was wrong I lent him books by Thurber and Benchley and the Grossmiths' *Diary of a Nobody*. Despite all this literature Yeats said he only smiled once—when Thurber's dog Muggs was put into the pantry with the mice during a party and lay there on the floor, growling to himself, not at the mice but about all the people in the next room that he would have liked to get at. Even 'The Secret Life of Walter Mitty' seemed to leave Jack Yeats unmoved. Perhaps the undertones in 'Walter Mitty' are too much on the tragic side, perhaps the same holds good of *The Diary of a Nobody*.

Michael also went to live in London and became a writer. He had graduated at Trinity College, Dublin, was called to the Irish Bar, decided not to practise law, became a schoolmaster in Hampstead for a while, then for some years worked on the London staff of the *Irish Times* writing the London Letter. In 1956 he produced his first novel, *Peter Perry*, a witty, sensitive and amusing book, it was followed by one in much the same style called *Oh Mary, this London*. His third was a satirical novel, *Across the Water*, about contemporary Dublin, which contains a charmingly perceptive por-trait of his father.

I once listened to Kot and James Stephens talking about English literature from Edmund Spenser to the present day. When Stephens and I got up to go, Stephens turned to me and said, 'The greatest book on English literature which has *never* been written is by Kot.'

Kot was always puzzled about writing in Ireland. He said the same language was used in England and it must have come from the same roots, the integrity of Milton, Bunyan and the rest; but when it came to Ireland it became 'fabricated', it lacked some quality of truth. He spoke of Yeats and Joyce and quoted Traherne: 'Things false are forced and most elaborate, Things pure and true are obvious unto sense.' He said, 'Yeats is the "epitome of the Irish People",' meaning something false and fabricated. He thought James Stephens's was the one original writing talent that had come out of Ireland.

I once said to Kot, 'You need a Boswell.' He said, 'You be my Boswell.' Then he added. 'When you quote me, you make me sound such a fool!' One afternoon at tea in Kot's kitchen, Juliette Huxley spoke of the work of a distinguished woman novelist. Kot said, 'Embroidery.' We tried to say that embroidery could be very good. Kot put his hands on the table with the palms facing each other and stared fixedly at the space between them as if he held something priceless there. He said, 'Literature is Holy Writ. If she wants to do embroidery, let her embroider her knickers.'

Kot used to say that Katherine was more interesting than her writing. For him Lawrence had the greatest and rarest talent that had appeared in our time. It was so easy to make fun of Lawrence—his rages, his snobbery, his pleasure in Frieda being 'a Baroness', his sewing and hemming, his trimming of hats. Kot even smiled at Katherine and Gertler's funny stories about Lawrence, but to Kot that side of him was so superficial as to be almost non-existent. An odd thing about Kot was the way that people whose lives impinged on the lives of his chosen ones became anathema to him. He had no love for Frieda or Murry or for James Stephens's wife, Cynthia.

Stephens's death was another great blow to Kot. It was shortly afterwards that Cynthia rang him and asked if she might go to him for some help and advice about James's affairs. I was there when she arrived. I had not seen her for years. She was still pretty and had the same original and attractive taste in clothes. Kot explained some legal point to her and gave her some advice. She then opened her handbag and pushed a piece of paper across the table towards him saying, 'See how he loved me.'

It was a short poem written to her by James when he was a young man, a lodger in her house in Dublin. I watched Kot as he read it. I saw he was deeply moved. In silence he handed it back to her. Cynthia passed it across the table to me. I read it, and was also moved by its simple, tender beauty. She put it back in her handbag and got up to go. I felt she had had a moment of triumph over Kot. When she was gone he went round throwing open windows and doors, and breathing heavily, he said, 'The very air is contaminated!' Kot's hates and prejudices were no ordinary emotions.

Life in Dublin went on much as usual after the Second World War. Jack Yeats began to achieve great importance as a painter, and his pictures were sold for large sums of money, sometimes running into thousands of pounds.

It became fashionable to be interested in painting. My painter friend Norah McGuinness and some like-minded young people started a rival show to the Royal Hibernian Academy. They called their show the Living Art Exhibition and held it once a year in the Gallery of the College of Art. It was mostly contemporary work. They had lectures, film shows and loan pictures from abroad, and did a lot to keep Irish painters in touch with foreign trends and movements. The society still keeps going successfully.

Some time after the Second World War I gave up going to London by boat and train. I found it so much quicker and pleasanter to fly. Kot was very interested in my accounts of flying, especially when I told him of the air hostesses. He liked the thought of a good-looking young woman in uniform, welcoming you into the plane, looking after you, bringing you refreshment and saying good-bye when you arrived at your destination. It was 'a new thing in travelling'.

On my visits to London I continued to give Kot long accounts of the theatres, cinemas and picture exhibitions I had been to. I once gave him an almost verbatim report of a sermon I had heard

182

in St Paul's preached by Dean Matthews. The subject was 'The Jews failed God'. It was not in any way against the Jews : in fact Dean Matthews, who was President of the London Society of Jews and Christians—if I remember rightly—gave a sympathetic explanation of how they had failed to live up to the extraordinarily high standards that they had set themselves.

Kot was very interested. He took a great pride in his race and maintained that even though they had failed God they had suffered for it. He spoke of the great literature of the Old Testament and the fairy tales of the New, and how churches are founded on fairy tales. He spoke of 'something distasteful' in the Christian idea of the 'Atonement'. He disliked organized religion; to him 'believers' and 'unbelievers' were different kinds of people, and he spoke of himself as an 'unbeliever'. He also disliked all accepted interpretations of the word 'God'.

As he spoke he seemed to explode all superstitions, annihilate all creeds and dogmas, in fact clear the air to such an extent that I felt I was no longer sitting at his kitchen table but was alone in some vast, empty, lonely space. He got up to put the kettle on the gas-stove. He must have been conscious of my feelings for he suddenly turned round and said, 'Mind you, Beatrice, in spite of all I say, I am God's most humble servant.' I was so surprised I nearly burst into tears. I knew he saw that I had some understanding of what he meant.

Kot had talked of immensities. Next day, when I arrived, he opened the door and said firmly, 'Today we will only gossip.' He disliked a lack of reticence in people and perhaps, on the previous afternoon, he felt he had revealed too much.

Kot once said jokingly, 'Ottoline wants to convert me.' He told me how she had persuaded him to go to St Paul's Cathedral with her. She thought he would be impressed by the beauty of the music and the Church of England service. The only feeling he got from it was one of absolute astonishment. It was all so completely Jewish; every hymn and psalm and prayer or reading from the Bible was about Jehovah, Jerusalem, the Children of Israel, Zion and the Hebrew prophets.

Kot would say, 'The B.B.C. has done Jesus Christ a lot of harm.'

I think he was alluding to the religious talks during Children's Hour—'Inferior minds explaining the inexplicable.' Perhaps as religious instruction for the children he would have preferred James Stephens's little poem 'Paternoster'.

> Do never pray,
> But only say
> —O Thou!
> And leave it so,
> For He will know
> —somehow—
> That you fall
> And that you call
> on Him now.

Kot was greatly impressed by Simone Weil as a writer deeply interested in religion. He had nothing but scorn for the religions of T. S. Eliot and Graham Greene, and of Dostoievsky he once said, 'Everything he touches he contaminates.'

I once asked Kot what was the most valuable thing to have in life. He said, 'A Real Human Relationship'; but that for such a thing it was also necessary to have a talent. It was not something you could arrive at by taking thought or making an effort, which left the unfortunate people who had no talent for such a thing in a sad way.

18

I rewrite a classic - Pomp in a cold climate - A blind man's Coronation Night - Murry recalls a debt - In the footsteps of Dean Swift - Kot refuses to listen - Last years of a dear friend - Explanations of an enigma - Thirty years of letter-writing rebound upon me - I build a bonfire

I would like all books to have happy endings. The happiest ending of any book I know is that of *The Vicar of Wakefield*. Misunderstandings are cleared up; families are united; people who are supposed to be dead are alive and well; everyone marries everyone else and they all become very rich. The book finishes as they all sit down to a great dinner at which the Vicar's wife 'has the pleasure of carving all the meat for all the company'. The Vicar writes: 'I can't say whether we had more wit among us now than usual, but I am certain we had more laughing which answered the end as well.' One jest so affected the 'two Miss Flamboroughs' that he thought they 'would have died with laughing'. He ends by saying that he has nothing now on this side of the grave to wish for; all his cares were over and his 'pleasure was unspeakable'.

Joe Hone once said he had never read *Villette*. I lent it to him but as I was afraid the sad ending would depress him I wrote a coda on the blank page at the end of the book, in which Lucy Snow, having written her last words, hears the door of her little room softly open and there before her is her beloved Professor, dripping with seaweed and sand, but safe and sound. He has survived the terrible storm that 'had strewn the Atlantic with wrecks and gorged the deeps with their full of sustenance'. In my version they both live together for years in a state of ecstatic happiness. Joe Hone liked my happy ending; I hope Charlotte Brontë forgives me.

My father-in-law had received a peerage in 1921, and after his death in 1931 Gordon succeeded to the title. Gordon took his seat in the House of Lords and we were duly allotted places on a sort of overflow peers' stand in Parliament Square for the coronation of Elizabeth II on 2 June, 1953. Michael and I, with a Canadian friend of his, Bill Holden, went to our seats early in the morning.

It was a terribly long, cold, wet day but it had its moments. One of them was when the pool of rainwater which had collected in the canvas roof over our heads burst the seams of the canvas and descended on us in a deluge. We survived, and saw the magnificent procession on its return journey from the Abbey. Though we were almost hysterical as a result of our suffering, we cheered madly with the rest of the vast crowd of people who were present. We even booed Dr Malan, though I think it passed unnoticed.

When the last of the marching regiments had gone from Parliament Square we took our special peers' train back to Cannon Street Station. London, outside the great barrier which contained the millions of onlookers, was a dead city—absolutely empty streets, a cat walking by itself, no human-being anywhere. We found a taxi and asked the driver if he could take us back to my hotel. He said with a grin, 'There's nothing to stop me.' The large hotel entrance hall was empty except for one porter leaning on a desk. The rest of the staff there had retired to the top floor, from which it was possible to get a glimpse of the procession, which was still on its way back to the palace with the roar of cheering going on and on incessantly.

Michael had gone back to the *Irish Times* office to write his London Letter for the paper. It was too late to go to Kot, so I dined alone. The restaurant was packed, but I got a small table to myself. At the next table there was an elderly military man in evening dress, wearing a lot of medals, and blind in both eyes. He had a woman with him who might have been his wife, and two younger people, a man and a woman. They all talked quietly to each other, except the blind man, who sat silently staring into space with sightless eyes. Everyone in the room seemed a bit subdued and exhausted. The early start and the cold and rain had been too much. There was no air of rejoicing.

The blind officer's wife helped him with his food. I felt that he was living in another world. Then he called the waiter and ordered champagne. When it was poured out he took his glass and stood up, saying in a strong voice, 'Her Majesty the Queen.' The members of his party stood up, looking rather embarrassed, and drank. The people at other tables looked round with curiosity, then turned again to their food. It was as if he was not there, but far away in some regimental mess with his comrades, or just alone in his dreams, with his medals, his blindness and his Queen.

Next day I went to Kot to tell him about our experience at the coronation. He had been very interested in the radio broadcast. His love of England included the Royal Family, although there was a time when he disapproved of the Princesses going to dances and night-clubs 'just like any other girl on the Finchley Road— Princesses should be different'.

For years we had lost touch with Murry. Kot sometimes had news of him, and we learnt that he had been married again, twice, and that both marriages were tragic and unhappy. Then we heard that he was running a sort of community farm in Norfolk and that he had met Mary Gamble, who became his fourth wife.

Murry was one of the people of whom Kot disapproved, but if he spoke against him he always added, 'Murry is a *real* writer, a *real* literary critic', which from Kot was high praise. In 1949 Murry wrote to me saying he had been asked to speak to the Trinity College Historical Society and was coming to Dublin. I asked him and Mary to come and stay with us. It was good to see him again; he had at one time been so much a part of our lives, and it was a relief to see him happy with Mary, who was the perfect wife for him.

It was about thirty years since we had seen Murry. Of course he looked different, but it was pleasant to note that some things about him had not changed : little mannerisms, the way he moved his hands when he spoke, his voice, his laugh, were all the same as when he was a young man. He had a strange trick while speaking of looking past you with each eye apparently fixed on a different corner of the ceiling, and as he spoke he seemed to draw his eyes

187

together. He always finished what he was saying with both eyes fixed intently on you.

Murry had always expressed a great devotion to Gordon since the faraway days of the great Dostoievsky discussions. One day he began to talk to me in a shy, embarrassed manner about some money which he said he had owed Gordon ever since those distant times. He said he had not forgotten about it, but for him the debt seemed like a bond between himself and Gordon. He felt that if he paid the debt the bond would be broken.

We both had a laugh as he said this; it seemed such a dubious kind of bond. I assured him that Gordon had looked on it as a privilege to have been able to help two young writers so worthy of being helped as he and Katherine, and said it would be better to forget the debt and leave the bond unbroken. It struck me that it was a bond that might have puzzled Polonius.

They came to Ireland again when Murry was writing his book on Swift. They brought their car to tour the country, loving it. Joe Hone and I went with them to St Patrick's cathedral to 'get the atmosphere' Dean de Pauley took us round the Deanery and all over the place, then we drove to Celbridge where Vanessa (Esther Vanhomrigh) had lived, where a gardener offered to show us the hide-out where Swift and Vanessa used to meet, in a grotto on a cliff overlooking the Liffey. The walk there seemed interminable, through gardens and fields and endless plantations of rhododendrons.

At last we arrived at the place and scrambled down the thickly wooded cliff to the little stone house. There was a stone seat across the back of it, just long enough to hold the four of us. We sat there, all very silent. The only sound was the river below running over the rocks, and the sudden rush of wings of birds disturbed by our presence. Perhaps we were all thinking the same thought— what had happened in that remote and secret place so long ago between that strange, passionate man and the beautiful young girl, twenty years his junior, so deeply in love with him? Perhaps also the idea had come into all our minds that they never met there at all; that the hide-out was a financial invention of the gardener's. The place *looked* authentic and it certainly had a haunted air.

I felt a bit like a traitor when I told Kot of our reunion with Murry. I did not know how he would take it, for he never seemed to understand how I could like anyone of whom he disapproved. He listened with great interest to my story, then asked if Murry ever spoke of Katherine. I said he did, but that he said the days of their association were 'all far away and long ago'. Kot said fiercely, 'Katherine is not far away and long ago, she is *here* and *now*.'

After Murry published Katherine's letters in 1951 Kot said to me, 'If you don't want to suffer pain, don't read the book.' I told him I had read it, and although it was painful, it was not intolerable, because her sufferings were all about herself. We were sitting at his kitchen table at the time, and he shrank back with a sort of jerk as if to avoid a blow. I realized that I had said a terrible thing.

I blundered on, trying to explain that to me pain which sprang from one's own unhappy love-affairs or one's own physical condition was bearable. It was the pain of knowing that a hair of the head of someone you loved was in danger, or that they were in pain, that was the unbearable kind of suffering. I knew that as Katherine's intense concentration on herself was partly the source of her art, that thought would help to make her pain tolerable. Kot would not listen. He said, 'No explanation is necessary.'

Next day, as I was leaving the house, he said, 'What you said about Katherine yesterday has shattered me.' Again I tried to explain. I wanted to discuss it with him, but he waved me away saying, 'Between us no explanations are necessary', which left me completely in the dark.

At one time during Kot's last years he asked me almost wistfully, 'Is Ireland beautiful?' It was as if he wanted to hear something to justify Ireland's existence. In his troubled mind, he still felt a contempt for Ireland for having been neutral during Hitler's horrible war.

When Kot began to suffer from his heart-trouble, a friend of his, Marjorie Wells, H. G. Wells's daughter-in-law, looked after him. She continued to do so, and for years was his most devoted nurse and care-taker. He spoke of her as 'his tower of strength'. She never seemed to weary, going backwards and forwards from her house to his every day for years, in all weathers. In the most tragic moments of his desperate illnesses she was with him, quietly helping, unsparingly giving of herself to his service. Another helper and good friend was Sophie Jacobs, whom I had known in Dublin as a girl, when she was Sophie Solomons.

During these last years Kot moved backwards and forwards from hospitals and nursing-homes to his house in Acacia Road. A couple of times he had been to a home where he had special treatment for his black moods. Sometimes he seemed much better, but his heart was not good and between heart-attacks and black moods life became unbearable for him.

I tried to cheer him by my accounts of our lovely home in the mountains, the beauty of Ireland and my happiness in having a little granddaughter, also by my persistent belief that everything would come right in the end; but his despair in the human condition and about himself had gone beyond my understanding. My visits did nothing to dispel his gloom.

It was as if all his queer hate and intolerance of other people had become centred on himself. He could not even forgive himself for being old and ill. His bitterness and resentment seemed to come from a sense of guilt and failure. He said, 'I have lived the sort of life I wanted to. I am paying for it now.' He always wanted to live quite alone and he valued his privacy greatly.

I know that one of the reasons for this feeling of guilt was that during the war years, when the housing shortage was so acute in London, Kot was living alone in a house with several vacant rooms. At one time he was compelled to let part of his house, but he hated the other people for being there and was greatly relieved when they left. He would have loved the house to have been kept as a museum or memorial to Katherine with himself as the keeper. He had Katherine's chair that she used when writing, a lock of her hair and a great number of her letters. In his will he left these letters, including a number of D. H. Lawrence's, to the British Museum; there were about 520 altogether.

I have wondered whether Kot felt defeated by his own aspirations for himself, and the sense that he knew he could never live up to them even in little things. Perhaps he felt he could have been a writer. There may have been something Oblomov-like in his laziness about making the effort to write. He found it easier to get up early in the morning, to scrub the floors, shake things in the garden and generally clean the house, humming gently to himself all the time.

Marjorie Wells rang me up from London, on 23 January 1955, to tell me of Kot's death. Murry wrote to me from his farm in Norfolk:

My dear Beatrice,

So Kot is dead. I saw the notice, by pure chance, in *The Times* on Monday last—a wildly inaccurate one; then later there was a fuller one, signed D.P. (which I assumed to be Dilys Powell) correcting the former mistakes but a little remote. I think I told you I met D.P. at a Blake dinner in November and we talked a little about Kot, in consequence of which I dallied with the thought of taking the risk of going to see him, but decided against it. Probably it was as well.

You will miss him very much. I am sorry for that. I, of course, had not seen him for more than 30 years. But in some way he is the more vivid for that; right from the first moment of my meeting him in the Lawrence cottage at Cholesbury in the autumn of 1914. You should write down, before it is too late, your abiding memories of him. Did he keep to his old strange locutions? 'She wants beating, *plainly*'—'He is a bli-ghter, plainly.' I see him always in massive profile, like some Sargon or Sennacherib on a bas-relief; a Semitic King of Kings, a monumental Rabbi, a Moses holding up or letting fall on some unfortunate— the tablets of the law.

If you do write down your memories of him, please let me see them.

Yours ever,

J.M.M.

Dilys Powell had for years been one of Kot's greatest friends.

191

In the article in *The Times* which Murry alluded to she wrote of his contribution to the world of letters by his translations and added: 'Those who knew him best may well feel that the most precious gift of all was his personal friendship, at once fierce and incorruptible, demanding always the absolute honesty it offered. Of not many is it said, "I am proud that he liked me." '

I wrote down some memories of Kot and sent them to Murry, who replied:

> That's lovely. *Please* go on. It's meat and drink to me. You see, quite apart from Kot's feeling about me, I was cut off—first by Katherine's then by Violet's illness. And when the last was over, I didn't belong anymore. The world of my old friends has become a strange world—another dimension from the world I lived in. And what you tell me helps me to bridge this queer gap in life.

Murry wrote again with a perhaps justifiable bitterness about Kot's influence on Katherine in relation to himself:

> Kot's view of our relation was quite superficial, and his relation to her was quite false. It consisted in making her up and sometimes she liked it, and sometimes she reacted against it because she knew I was being made the scapegoat, and since in her heart of hearts she recognized that was unfair, a kind of treachery, she couldn't accept the position he wanted to thrust upon her. As a matter of fact Kot's influence upon her was quite pernicious. The one chance of saving (or prolonging) her life was in her staying quiet with me in Switzerland. He filled her with the dangerous dream of being completely cured by the Russian, Manoukhin, from the inevitable failure of which she reacted into the spiritual quackery of Gurdjieff—and death. Katherine was lovely—much lovelier than Kot ever knew. Her suffering, which was great, came not through me, but from herself. Kot fed what was false in her, and what she knew was false. Knowing what I know, it would have been impossible for Kot and me to be friends, without my telling him the truth. He *would never* have taken it. He didn't like truth. It was not his kind of meat.

THE INTRUDER by Beatrice Glenavy, RHA, 1933

PRIMULA by Beatrice Glenavy, RHA, 1953

PAPER by Beatrice Glenavy, RHA, 1962

THE DANCING MEN by Beatrice Glenavy, RHA, 1962

Violet Schiff and I also wrote to each other about Kot, trying to explain and understand his strange contradictions. In one of her letters she said:

I see him now as a bewildered innocent, arriving a stranger in this country, barely able to speak the language and soon taken up by a group of highly gifted people who did not understand him and whom he did not understand, though he was unaware of it. He was dazzled by them, but with few exceptions they had no real friendship or affection for him. They liked and admired him, he was welcomed as a stimulating novelty. Among Kot's various laudable ambitions was a great wish to exercise a good influence on others. You have exposed, perhaps unwittingly, the unreality and shallowness of some of his relationships, not on his side as he was a simple truly honest man and hated all pretence and humbug. He may have been confused and distressed by the inconsistencies and complexity he saw in his associates. Then later, with the frustration of his personal aims and hopes, he got more and more discouraged and began to hate most people he met. I attribute this to his not understanding them, for he was fundamentally benevolent, kind and anxious to help everyone.

I have looked up letters from Lawrence to Gordon and myself to see if he says anything about Kot. In a letter to Gordon dated 25 January 1917, written from Zennor in Cornwall, I find the following:

You exasperate me almost to contempt, still the liking doesn't change. Murry fills me with loathing, still somehow I am fond of him. Kot wearies me to extinction and yet I couldn't forego him.

Marjorie Wells had the sad job of clearing up Kot's house and getting rid of his belongings. She wrote to ask me what I would like done with my letters.

I had written to him about once a week for thirty years. Kot himself was almost incapable of writing letters, which I found terribly hard to understand, especially when he told me that he had hardly written to his mother, whom he loved, from the time he left Russia till her death. He knew what happiness a letter from him could give her and how she must have longed for news of him. I believe he suffered very much from the thought of this.

Kot only wrote to me if he had something important to tell me. He used to ask me to go on writing even if I never heard from him because he looked forward so much to the one day in the week when the postman handed my letter through the kitchen window; even the postman was distressed if my letter was a day late.

I asked Marjorie Wells to send my letters back to me. For about a week large cardboard boxes kept arriving every day, closely packed with my letters in their envelopes. I was horrified; I was overwhelmed; I tried to read them but could not bear it. They were covered with the *cœur de lion* dust. I soaked them in turpentine and took them out to the garden and burnt them.

It is extremely difficult to burn letters. They blaze up and you think they are finished, for all look black. With a long stick you begin to poke and prod the black ashes, then masses of writing-paper untouched by fire keep appearing. I thought of Lucy Snow burying her letters from Dr John (how easy that seemed) or Hedda Gabler burning Eilert Lovborg's manuscript without any trouble at all. By the end of the week I was exhausted, but still the letters came.

I remember Katherine once told me how she had walked and talked with Rupert Brooke after he was dead. She said it was a game that she often played by herself, walking and talking with the dead, and sometimes it was very pleasant. I found that I too could play that game. As I worked at the burning of my letters I felt that Kot was with me. I said, 'A nice job you have left me. I told you to burn my letters. Why did you keep them?' He explained, 'I did not think they were literature. I kept them because they were a sort of history of the time and might be useful to anyone writing about it.' I told him to get another long stick from the heap of pea-stakes and help me to poke the bonfire. He did, and we worked happily together in peace. It was rather fun when both our sticks caught fire.

Index